On Drink is a layman's guide to the labyrinths of alcoholic lore which lie around us. As well as three useful and refreshingly debunking chapters on wine, there is a wealth of cocktail recipes of varying potency. For those who are forced to entertain against their preferences, Kingsley Amis presents an invaluable and hilarious 'Mean Sod's Guide (incorporating Mean Slag's Guide)'. The book also covers such items as the necessities which should be kept in the cellar or the larder, what to drink with what, bar equipment and indeed all requirements for the civilized entertainment of one's friends and, of course, oneself!

'Much sound advice . . . exceedingly funny'
Oxford Mail

'Entertaining . . . downright practical as well'
Signature – Diners Club Journal

D1471442

Also by Kingsley Amis in Panther Books

I Want It Now
The Green Man
What Became of Jane Austen? and other questions
Girl, 20
*That Uncertain Feeling**
*I Like It Here**

* Forthcoming

Kingsley Amis

On Drink

*Nicolas Bentley
drew the pictures*

Panther

Granada Publishing Limited
Published in 1974 by Panther Books Ltd
Frogmore, St Albans, Herts AL2 2NF

First published in Great Britain by
Jonathan Cape Ltd 1972
Text © 1970 and 1972 by Kingsley Amis and
the *Daily Telegraph*. Illustrations ©
1972 by Nicolas Bentley
Made and printed in Great Britain by
Richard Clay (The Chaucer Press) Ltd
Bungay, Suffolk
Set in Monotype Ehrhardt

Some parts of this book appeared, in a slightly different form, in
the *Daily Telegraph Magazine*.

Contents

To Pat and George Gale

ON DRINK

Introduction

Anthropologists assure us that wherever we find man he speaks. Chimpanzee-lovers notwithstanding, no animal other than man is capable of laughter. And, although some undiscovered tribe in the Brazilian jungle might conceivably prove an exception tomorrow, every present-day society uses alcohol, as have the majority of those of the past. I am not denying that we share other important pleasures with the brute creation, merely stating the basic fact that conversation, hilarity and drink are connected in a profoundly human, peculiarly intimate way.

There is a choice of conclusions from this. One would be that no such healthy linkage exists in the case of other drugs: a major reason for being on guard against them. More to the point, the collective social benefits of drinking altogether (on this evidence) outweigh the individual disasters it may precipitate. A team of American investigators concluded recently that, without the underpinning provided by alcohol and the relaxation it affords, Western society would have collapsed irretrievably at about the time of the First World War. Not only is drink here to stay; the moral seems to be that when it goes, we go too.

It has certainly increased its hold on our lives with the world-wide move to the towns and the general increase in prosperity. Wine and beer are—in origin, in the countries that produce them—drinks of the village and the poorer classes; gin and whisky belong to the city and, these days at any rate, the rather better off. In other words, our drinks are getting stronger as well as more numerous.

The strains and stresses of urban living, to coin a phrase, are usually held accountable for these increases. I should not dissent from this exactly, but I should single out one stress (or strain) as distinctly more burdensome, and also more widespread, than most: sudden confrontation with complete or comparative strangers in circumstances requiring a show of relaxation and amiability—an experience that I, for one, never look forward to without misgiving, even though I nearly always turn out to enjoy it in the event. While the village remained the social unit, strangers appeared seldom, and when they did were heavily outnumbered by your family, your friends, people you had known all your life. Nowadays, in the era of the business lunch, the dinner party, the office party, the anything-and-everything party, strangers pour over the horizon all the time.

The reason why I, and most others, usually turn out to enjoy meeting such creatures is simply and obviously the co-presence of drink. The human race has not devised any way of dissolving barriers, getting to know the other chap fast, breaking the ice, that is one-tenth as handy and efficient as letting you and the other chap, or chaps, cease to be totally sober at about the same rate in agreeable surroundings. Well and good, the serious student of the effects of drink will retort in the grim, curmudgeonly tone peculiar to serious students of the effects of drink; well and good, but what about what happens later? What about those who drink, not to cease to be totally sober, but to get drunk? What about the man who drinks *on his own*?

Well, what about it and them and him? I have nothing to offer, nothing more to add to serious sociological speculation about the whys and wherefores of indulgence in alcohol. Or only this: leaving aside dipsomaniacs, most or many of whom are born, not made, I feel that there is very little we can safely add, in discussing our motives for drinking, to the verdict of the poet who said we do it because 'we are dry, or lest we may be by and by, or any other reason why'.

Where and what and how we drink, or should drink, are different and more interesting questions. As to where, this is so much a matter of individual preference and geographical opportunity that I should drop it right away, except that it gives me a long-sought chance to deliver a short, grouchy blast against what has been done, and what is still being done, to that deeply, traditionally British drinking centre, the pub.

With some shining exceptions, of which my own local is one, the pub is fast becoming uninhabitable. Fifteen or twenty years ago, the brewing companies began to wake up to the fact that their pubs badly needed a face-lift, and started spending millions of pounds to bring them up to date. Some of the results of their refurbishings have been admirable: more and more comfortable seating, improved hygiene, chilled beers, snack lunches that in general have reached such a standard that, when in quest of a midday meal in unfamiliar territory, you will usually find quicker service and much better value for money in the pub than in the near-by trattoria.

But that is about as far as it goes. The interior of today's pub has got to look like a television commercial, with all the glossy horror that implies. Repulsive 'themes' are introduced: the British-battles pub, ocean-liner pub, Gay Nineties pub. The draught beer is no longer true draught, but keg, that hybrid substance that comes out of what is in effect a giant metal bottle, engineered so as to be the same everywhere, no matter how lazy or incompetent the licensee, and, in the cases of at least two well-known, lavishly advertised brews, pretty nasty everywhere. But all this could be put up with cheerfully enough if it were not for the bloody *music* — or that kind of uproar having certain connections with a primitive style of music and known as pop. It is not really the pop as such that I object to, even though pop is very much the sort of thing that I, in common with most of the thirty- or thirty-five-plus age-group, would have expected to go to the pub to get away from. For partly different reasons, I should also object to having Beethoven's Choral Symphony blaring away while I tried to enjoy a quiet pint with friends. If you dislike what is being played, you use up energy and patience in the attempt to ignore it; if you like it, you will want to listen to it and not to talk or be talked to, not to do what you came to the pub largely to do.

I have always understood that pop and popular music came to pubs because the brewers hoped thereby to reverse the falling-off in the recruitment of younger patrons noticeable in the post-war period. If I am right in that assumption, then they were wrong in theirs. Pop not only tends to drive the older customer out; it fails to attract, and even keeps away, large sections of the young, including some who welcome pop *on its own ground*. (I wonder very much what would be the effect on the trade of a publican who put up a notice at his door saying, 'No Music Inside'. Will someone try it?) Anyway, we pay the pipers; we ought to be able to call the absence of tunes.

Until we can, many of us will prefer to drink in our own or our friends' homes. But here too, certainly in the homes of more than one or two friends of mine, the fairly serious, reasonably discriminating drinker can find plenty to offend him without having to look at all far. What most often springs to his eye is not being given enough. Those of us who are poor or mean cannot or will not do much about this. But for the benefit of those who are neither, who have merely got their priorities wrong, let me enunciate

G.P. (General Principle) 1: *Up to a point (i.e. short of offering your guests one of those Balkan plonks marketed as wine, Cyprus sherry, poteen and the like), go for quantity rather than quality. Most people would rather have two glasses of ordinary decent port than one of a rare vintage. On the same reasoning, give them big drinks rather than small—with exceptions to be noted later. Serious drinkers will be pleased and reassured, unserious ones will not be offended, and you will use up less chatting-time going round to recharge glasses.*

My final observation, before getting down to details, is that serving good drinks, like producing anything worth while, from a poem to a motor-car, is troublesome and expensive. (If you are interested, a worthwhile poem is expensive to the poet in the sense that he could almost always earn more money by spending the time on some other activity.) But I undertake, in what follows, to keep a sharp eye on both points, to show where and how trouble can be minimized and to what degree you can legitimately cut down costs.

It is the unbroken testimony of all history that alcoholic liquors have been used by the strongest, wisest, hand-somest, and in every way best races of all times.

GEORGE SAINTSBURY

'If I had a thousand sons, the first human principle I would teach them should be, to forswear thin potations.' — WILLIAM SHAKESPEARE (Falstaff, *Henry IV, Part 2*)

There's nought, no doubt, so much the spirit calms
  As rum and true religion.

LORD BYRON

Drinking
Literature

One infallible mark of your true drink-man is that he reads everything on the subject that comes his way, from full-dress books to those tiny recipe-leaflets the makers tend to hang round the necks of their bottles. Never, by the way, despise the latter sort of thing as a mere commercial hand-out; on the contrary, the manufacturer knows more about his product than anybody else and, never mind from what base motives, will have tested out his recommendations with the utmost care. These days, too, off-licence price-lists can offer a lot of straight information.

This policy of unsleeping vigilance will bring you useful tips outside the common run: I have forgotten where I read that you can get much more juice out of a lemon you have dumped in a bowl of warm water for a few minutes than out of one straight from the fruit-bowl, let alone from anywhere cold, but it is true, and I always follow this advice myself when making a Bloody Mary (for instance) and have the time and patience. On the other hand, the books are full of lore that you will only very rarely, if ever, have the chance of translating into practice. I think of such attractive fantasies as the recipe given in *The Art of Mixing Drinks* (based on *Esquire Drink Book*) for Admiral Russell's Punch. This starts off by inviting the mixer to get hold of four hogsheads of brandy, and explains that a hogshead is 63 gallons—U.S. gallons: the equivalent is something over

The legend of the label

50 British gallons, or 300-plus bottles. Included, along with such items as five pounds of grated nutmeg, is the juice of 2,500 lemons, warmth or coldness not specified. My calculation is that the totality (a lot of wine goes into it too) will serve 2,000 guests for a more-intensive-than-average evening party, or alternatively six people for a year-round piss-up. Try the latter some time and let me know how you get on, if you can. Pick your company with care.

More practically, you will waste a lot of time—unless of course you are simply using your drinks manual as dipsography, the alcoholic equivalent of pornography—reading about concoctions that call for stuff you simply have not got to hand. You may like the sound of a Grand Slam as prescribed in *The Diners' Club Drink Book*, with its jigger of Carioca rum, whatever that is, its half-jiggers of brandy and Curaçao, its dash of Kirschwasser and the rest, but, professional bartenders and fanatical booze-collectors apart, you are likely to have to read on in search of something you can make from stock. (A way of reducing this problem is outlined in my note on The Store Cupboard.)

Most drink-men, however, will like to feel they have on their shelves an authoritative and reasonably comprehensive encyclopedia of liquor, and the present little book, although needless to say frighteningly authoritative, is, for reasons explained elsewhere, not comprehensive, at least so far as its recipes are concerned. *The Fine Art of Mixing Drinks*, by David A. Embury (Faber), scores high from this point of view, and is written in a pleasantly companionable style. It is also—inevitably—American, which slightly diminishes its usefulness in the British context, and the author is what I shall venture to call *wrong* here and there, but his book is without doubt your Best Buy. Of shorter guides of this kind, I would recommend *3 Bottle Bar*, by H.i.—Yes, i. No, I don't know—Williams (Faber). Both are in paperback.

Neither Embury nor Williams has much to say about wine, except as regards its role in hot or cold punches and the like. Their business is with cocktails, coolers, cobblers, cups; with mixed drinks, in fact. Very few people who are proficient in this field know or care anything about wine as such, and the same applies in reverse to wine men. As the reader will see, I am not much of a wine man, but some of my best friends are, and I have called in expert assistance to guide me here.

The *Easy Guide to Wine*, issued free by the Wine Development Board (6 Snow Hill, London ECI), will tell the beginner most of what he wants to know in its couple of dozen pages of sound, well-chosen information and advice. For the more advanced, or more inquisitive, Alexis Lichine's *Encyclopedia of Wines and Spirits* and all other alcoholic drinks too (Cassell) is very solidly professional and factual, laying much greater stress on wines than on spirits: it devotes more space to Gevrey-Chambertin, one of thirty wine-producing districts in part of Burgundy, than to gin. *Wines and Spirits of the World*, edited by Alec H. Gold (Virtue), is similarly comprehensive and equally wine-oriented, but with a lot of splendid photographs thrown in. A real dipsographic debauch, so much so that I had to struggle with my better nature for quite a few seconds before deciding to add, lifemanfully, that I did note one or two omissions: no mention is made of the wines of New York State, with their annual yield comparable to that of Cyprus ... But those who, like me, have tasted some of the wines of New York State will find it hard to care. Lastly, *The Penguin Book of Wines*, by Allan Sichel, is an excellent cheap guide: unpretentious, thorough (300 pages) and very practical, quoting plenty of names and up-to-date (1971) prices.

With all these books, as with any on the subject, do not

expect to turn yourself into an expert via the printed word alone. You can commit to memory everything Lichine has to say about Gevrey-Chambertin and still have no idea whether you would like the wine. Reading must be combined with as much drinking experience as pocket and liver will allow.

One final recommendation. You need not take the slightest interest in any of these matters to get a lot out of *Cocktail Party Secrets*, by Vernon Heaton (Elliot Right Way Books). The title set me off on fantasies about martinis based on industrial alcohol, whisky sours spiked with LSD, etc. And I was hooked by the bold opening statement, offered by way of answer to the equally challenging question, 'Why a Cocktail Party?', that serves as title of the first chapter:

> Everybody, on occasion,
> (*a*) wants to,
> (*b*) feels they [*sic*] ought to,
> (*c*) or have [*sic*] reason to
> entertain their [*sic*] friends in their [*sic*] own homes [*sic*].

The author goes on to suggest reasons why people should get these ideas, such as that they enjoy parties, or want to return a party given by someone else at *his* home. In the same ground-covering style, he points out that parties can be small or large; that they require preparation but that bottles can be lined up in advance; that you must decide (*a*) who you *want* to invite, (*b*) who you *think* should come, (*c*) who you feel you *must* invite, (*d*) who you think it is *politic* to invite; that, where possible, cloakroom facilities should be available; and much, much more. My word, if these are secrets, what can be the like of the publicly available information on the topic that has been lying about unregarded all these years?

I must get hold of the same writer's *Wedding Etiquette Properly Explained* and *The Best Man's Duties*. I can see it now — 'People get married because (*a*) they *want* to, (*b*) they feel they *ought* to, (*c*) somebody is *pointing a shotgun* at them ... '

To make cock ale: Take ten gallons of ale and a large cock, the older the better; Parboil the cock, flay him, and stamp him in a stone mortar till his bones are broken (you must craw and gut him when you flay him), then put the cock into two quarts of sack [sweet or sweetish white wine], and put it to three pounds of raisins of the sun stoned, some blades of mace and a few cloves; put all these into a canvas bag, and a little before you find the ale has done working, put the ale and bag together into a vessel; in a week or nine days bottle it up, fill the bottles but just above the neck, and give it the same time to ripen as other ale. — Old recipe given in F. C. Lloyd's *Art and Technique of Wine*

To sweeten musty casks: Take some dung of a milking cow when it is fresh, and mix it with a quantity of warm water, so as to make it sufficiently liquid to pass through a funnel, but previously dissolve two pounds of bay salt and one pound of alum; then put the whole in a pot on the fire, stir it with a stick and when nearly boiling, pour it into the cask, bung it up tight, shake it about, and let it remain in for two hours, then give it another stirring and after two hours more it may be rinsed out with cold water. — Prescription quoted in F. C. Lloyd's *Art and Technique of Wine*

Actual Drinks

I provide here only a selection. A complete account of all known drinks, from absinthe to the Zoom cocktail (brandy, honey and cream—not today, thank you) would be deadening to write and read. Completeness would also involve the rehearsal of a good deal of common knowledge. It would be rather shabby to take money for explaining that, for instance, a gin and tonic consists of gin and tonic, plus ice and a slice of lemon. However, this gives me occasion to remark that that admittedly excellent and refreshing drink gains an extra thirst-quenching tang from a good squeeze of lemon juice in addition to the lemon slice, and so to propound

    🍷G.P. 2: *Any drink traditionally accompanied by a bit of fruit or vegetable is worth trying with a spot of the juice thrown in as well.*

I confine myself, then, to giving recipes intended to offer something of my own, whether it be a modest tip like the one exemplified above, an attack on some received notion, or, as in some cases, a whole new formula—if there is any such thing in a field so extensively and intensively studied. What follows is the fruit of some dozen years' research; I started drinking much longer ago, be in no doubt of that, but had to reach a certain stage of affluence before I could risk spoiling even a mouthful of liquor by foolhardy experiment. My three categories are the Short and the Long and the Hot, an illogical but, there being no short hot drinks, practical mode of division.

SHORT DRINKS

If, as Philip Larkin observed not so long ago, the age of jazz (not the same thing as the Jazz Age) ran roughly from 1925 to 1945, the age of the cocktail covered the same sort of period, perhaps starting a little earlier and taking longer to die away finally. The two were certainly associated at their inception. Under Prohibition in the United States, the customer at the speakeasy drank concoctions of terrible liquor and other substances added in order to render the result just about endurable, while the New Orleans Rhythm Kings or the Original Memphis Five tried to take his mind further off what he was swallowing. The demise of jazz cannot have had much to do with that of the cocktail, which probably faded away along with the disappearance of servants from all but the richest private houses. Nearly every cocktail needs to be freshly made for each round, so that you either have to employ a barman or find yourself constantly having to quit the scene so as to load the jug. Straight drinks are quicker, and guests can— indeed, often do—help themselves to them.

The Dry Martini and its variants have hung on longer than most. In this case it is possible to make up a large quantity beforehand and keep it chilled; but there are several snags to this procedure. The main part of the standard refrigerator is not cold enough to keep the drink cold enough for more than half an hour at the outside, and the ice-making compartment of such a refrigerator is not tall enough to hold any decent-sized jug. (You can muck about with teacups and such if you like, but this will take you about as long as mixing fresh.) A deep freeze will keep the drinks cold enough as long as anybody could want, but, again, you must put your jug back in it the moment you have finished pouring each new round, and this will probably involve you in a good deal of walking to and fro. And most experts will tell you that the bloom begins to fade from a martini as soon as it is first mixed, which may be pure subjectivism, but, in any drinking context, subjectivism is very important. No, I am sorry, but the only way to give your guests first-rate martinis without trouble to yourself is to take them to a first-rate cocktail bar. At home, you will just have to grit your teeth and get down to it, as follows:

The Dry Martini

12 to 15 parts gin
1 part dry vermouth
Lemon rind or cocktail onions
Ice cubes

A couple of hours before the party, get your glasses together. These should be on the small side—the second half of a too-large martini will have become too warm by the time the average drinker gets to it—and have some sort of stem or base to prevent the hand imparting warmth. (Like Glass No. 2 in the list below, page 49.) Fill each with water and put it in the refrigerator.

With, say, fifteen minutes to go, make an honest attempt at the fiendish task of cutting off some little strips of lemon rind so thinly that you take off none of the white pith underneath. Fill—and I mean fill—your jug with ice and pour in the gin and the vermouth, enough for one round, i.e. about one bottle of gin for every ten guests. (You will soon learn to judge the proportion of vermouth by

24

eye.) Stir vigorously for about a minute. Leave to stand for two to three minutes. The books are against this, remarking truly that you will be allowing the ice to melt further and so dilute the mixture, but it does make the result appreciably colder; which leads me straight to

✹G.P. 3: *It is more important that a cold drink should be as cold as possible than that it should be as concentrated as possible.*

While the jug is standing, empty the water out of the glasses and drop a bit of lemon rind in each. If you can face it, try squeezing the rind over the glass first to liberate the pungent oil within. There is a knack to this which I have never mastered. Partly for this reason, I prefer to substitute a cocktail onion for the rind.

Stir again for a few seconds and pour. If there is any liquor left over, you have my permission to put it in the refrigerator for use in the next round, provided you remove every particle of ice beforehand.

Notes. (i) Use Booth's dry gin, the yellow sort. White gin is for long drinks—with tonic, bitter lemon, etc.

(ii) Use Martini e Rossi dry vermouth. Noilly Prat darkens the drink, making it look less dry than it is, and is too strongly flavoured. (However, it is probably the best dry vermouth for drinking on its own.)

(iii) In pursuit of G.P. 3, stand by with ice cubes, to rechill the partly drunk drinks of any rotters or slackers who may opt out of later rounds.

(iv) Experts will say that I have described, not a dry martini, but its drier derivative, the Gibson, which does substitute an onion for the true martini's lemon rind. Well, yes, but few people, I think, who have sampled the formula I give, by which the vermouth flavour disappears as such and yet the total flavour is still not at all that of straight gin, will want to return to the 4:1 or 3:1 ratios prescribed by convention. And my version is stronger.

The Lucky Jim

12 to 15 parts vodka
1 part dry vermouth
2 parts cucumber juice
Cucumber slices
Ice cubes

For this derivative of the Vodka Gibson, proceed as for the Dry Martini where appropriate. The cucumber juice can be made quite simply, though not without some effort, by cutting off a chunk, or series of chunks, about two inches long and applying first one end, then the other, to an ordinary manual lemon-squeezer. Sieve the result through a coffee-strainer into your mixing-jug on top of the liquor and ice, give an extra thorough stirring, and serve. What you serve should be treated with respect, not because it is specially strong but because it tastes specially mild and bland. It looks unusual, rather mysterious in fact: faintly coloured and faintly cloudy, the green wine of the Chinese emperors come to vigorous life. For visual reasons, the cucumber slice you float on top of each glass should have its peel left on.

Notes. (i) Use a British vodka, the cheapest you can find, in pursuance of

> 🐟 G.P. 4: *For any liquor that is going to be mixed with fruit juices, vegetable juices, etc., sweetening, strongly flavoured cordials and the like, go for the cheapest reliable article. Do not waste your Russian or Polish vodka, etc.*

(ii) The character after whom I have named this drink would probably make his Clement Freud face if offered one, but he would be among the first to appreciate that its apparent mildness might make it an excellent love-philtre to press on shy young ladies, if there are any of these left anywhere in the land.

The Copenhagen

4 or 5 parts vodka
1 part Danish akvavit
Blanched almonds
Ice cubes

Proceed as before, dropping an almond into each glass as you serve. Wondering what the almond is doing there (I believe it is a Scandinavian good-luck token) will keep your guests' tongues wagging until the liquor sets them wagging about anything under the sun. Distilled out at 79° proof, akvavit is a strong drink, so much so that it seems to extend its power over the whole.

The following short drinks are best prepared by the glass, not in quantity.

The Pink Gin

Yes, yes, gin and half a dozen drops—no more—of Angostura bitters and some ice. But see that the gin is Booth's (my choice) or Plymouth (preferred by most other authorities), and, for a quick kick, dilute with Perrier or Apollinaris if you can afford it, soda water if not, rather than plain water. This takes account of

G.P. 5: *The alcohol in any bubbly drink will reach you faster than in its still version. Hence, or partly hence, the popularity of champagne at weddings and other festivities.*

Drop a cocktail onion in each glass, and, acting on G.P. 2, try adding a few drops of the solution the onions have been pickled in. The Pink Gin is a rather démodé drink well worth reviving. It is also, of course, a long drink if you add a lot of soda. Better not.

The Gin (or Vodka) and Orange or Peach Bitters

2 parts gin (or vodka)
1 part orange or peach bitters
Ice cubes

I include this not because I can claim to have invented it, but because not many people seem to know that orange and peach bitters exist. They are not, these days, very easy to come by, but your supplier should be able to order them for you. They are bitters in the dilute, Campari sense, not in the concentrated, Angostura sense. Mixing them with gin (or vodka) gives a pleasing alternative to the standard short gin (or vodka) drinks.

The Salty Dog

1 part gin
2 parts fresh grapefruit juice
Salt
Ice cubes

Take two saucers and fill one with plain water, the other with table salt. Moisten the rim of each glass and then twirl it about in the salt, so that it picks up a thickish coating about a quarter of an inch deep. Carefully add the gin and juice, stir, add ice, stir, and drink through the band of salt. You either like it or not.

The MacCossack

Equal parts of vodka and green ginger wine poured over ice. Very good if you like ginger wine (and vodka). I do.

The Kingers
2 parts montilla
1 part fresh orange juice
1 small shake Angostura bitters
Ice cubes

Montilla is a lightly fortified wine from Spain, similar to sherry (as the sherry-growers, a couple of hundred miles down the road, have often taken advantage of noticing in an unproductive year), but nuttier: well worth drinking, chilled, on its own. The present drink is a sort of cobbler — if you think that means it will mend your shoes, you are wrong. Just mix everything together, stir with ice, remove the ice and serve.

The Dizzy Lizzy
4 oz. Chambéry
1 teaspoon framboise
1 teaspoon cognac
1 small shake Angostura bitters
Ice cubes

Chambéry is the classiest French vermouth, and framboise a fine raspberry liqueur. Both are very drinkable on their own, framboise with caution. Mix with ice, remove ice and serve. Named, not *all that* inappropriately, after its deviser, my wife.

Queen Victoria's Tipple

½ *tumbler red wine*
Scotch

I have it on the authority of Colm Brogan that the Great Queen was 'violently opposed to teetotalism, consenting to have one cleric promoted to a deanery only if he promised to stop advocating the pernicious heresy', and that the above was her dinner-table drink, 'a concoction that startled Gladstone'—as I can well believe.

The original recipe calls for claret, but anything better than the merely tolerable will be wasted. The quantity of Scotch is up to you, but I recommend stopping a good deal short of the top of the tumbler. Worth trying once.

Scholars will visualize, pouring in the whisky, the hand of John Brown, the Queen's Highland servant, confidant and possibly more besides; and I for one, if I listen carefully, can hear him muttering, 'Och, Your Majesty, dinna mak' yoursel' unweel wi' a' yon parleyvoo moothwash—ha'e a wee dram o' guid malt forbye.' Or words to that effect.

The Old-Fashioned

Theoretically, one should be able to make up a lot of this in advance, but I have never done so successfully. For each drink, then, take

1 huge slug bourbon whiskey (say 4 fl. oz.)
1 level teaspoon castor sugar

As little hot water as will dissolve the
sugar completely
3 dashes Angostura bitters
1 hefty squeeze of fresh orange juice
1 teaspoon maraschino-cherry juice
1 slice orange
1 maraschino cherry
3 ice cubes

This is far less complicated and bothersome than it may look, and the result is the only cocktail really to rival the martini and its variants. Put the dissolved sugar into a glass, add the bitters, the juices and the whiskey, and stir furiously. Add the ice cubes and stir again. Lastly, push the orange slice down alongside the ice, drop in the cherry, and serve. You may supply drinking-straws if it is that sort of party.

Note. You really have to use bourbon. The Rye Old-Fashioned is not too bad; the Irish version just tolerable; the Scotch one not worth while.

The (whiskey) Manhattan
4 parts bourbon whiskey
1 part Italian (red) vermouth
1 dash or so Angostura bitters
1 maraschino cherry
Ice cubes

As above, stir the fluids together very hard before adding the ice and fruit. Whatever the pundits may say, this is in practice the not very energetic man's Old-Fashioned, and is an excellent drink, though never, I think, as good as a properly made Old-Fashioned. As above, again, or even more so, you really have to use bourbon.

The Iberian

1 part Bittall
1 part very dry sherry
1 orange slice
Ice cubes

You can surely see how to make this. Bittall is a Portuguese
wine apéritif consisting in effect of light (i.e. non-heavy) port
flavoured with orange-peel. I myself find it delicious on its
own — serve well chilled — but some will find it a little on the
sweet side for a pre-meal drink: mixing it with the sherry
offsets this. (See also under Hot Drinks, below.) It is not
on general sale, but your wine merchant can get it for you.

I can hardly stop you if you decide to make your guests
seem more interesting to you and to one another by mixing
in a shot of vodka.

The Normandy

1 slug calvados (2 fl. oz.)
1 dose champagne cider (about 3 fl. oz.)
1 dash Angostura bitters
1 level teaspoon castor sugar
As little hot water as will dissolve the
sugar completely
1 apple slice
Ice cubes

Put the dissolved sugar, the bitters and the calvados into
a glass and stir furiously. Add ice and stir furiously.
Remove ice, add chilled cider, drop in apple slice, and serve.

Note. Connoisseurs will already have sussed that this
longish short drink is a translation of the orthodox cham-

pagne cocktail, based on brandy and champagne, out of grape into apple. They should also have sussed that it is substantially cheaper: calvados is a few shillings dearer than a three-star cognac, but champagne cider is a quarter the price of even the very cheapest champagne. This cocktail tends to go down rather faster than its strength warrants; I have had heads in the soup when offering it as an apéritif.

The Tigne Rose

1 tot gin
1 tot whisky
1 tot rum
1 tot vodka
1 tot brandy

Even if you keep the tots small, which is strongly advisable, this short drink is not very short. It owes its name to Tigne Barracks, Malta, where it was offered as a Saturday lunch-time apéritif in the Sergeants' Mess of the 36th Heavy A.A. Regt., R.A., to all newly joined subalterns. The sometime 2nd Lieut. T. G. Rosenthal, R.A., from whom I had the recipe, says he put down three of them before walking unaided back to his room and falling into a reverie that lasted until Monday-morning parade. A drink to dream of, not to drink.

LONG DRINKS

There is no need to wax sociological over these. You must, however, try to observe

G.P. 6: *With drinks containing fruit (other than the decorative or olfactory slice of lemon, orange, etc.) it is really worth while to soak the fruit in some of the liquor for at least three hours beforehand.*

Everything else is *ad libitum*, as can be seen from this recipe for

Generic Cold Punch

A lot of cheap medium-dry wine, white, red or rosé—your wine merchant will help you choose
Some vodka—the quantity depending on your pocket and how drunk you intend your guests to become, but not more than one-quarter of the quantity of wine
A glass or two of some relatively non-sticky liqueur—optional
A load of any fresh fruit that happens to be about—peaches and strawberries are best
Ice cubes

Cut up the fruit and put it in some sort of bowl—anything from a tureen to a baby's bath will do. Pour some of the wine over it and leave to stand as under G.P. 6. When the party approaches, add the rest of the drink and stir thoroughly. The best method of serving is via your jug—with luck you will be able to fill this by submerging it bodily in the bowl, though it is worth taking out and throwing back any chunks of fruit that have got into the jug. Soaked fruit looks nasty. (If you want to do the thing in style, you will have a fresh supply of fruit to go in the individual glasses.) Now, no sooner, is the time to introduce ice. Stir the punch and the ice *in the jug* and start pouring, keeping ice out of the glasses.

Stern application of G.P. 4 makes any such potion inexpensive, but the best value for money of the lot, and a very pleasant medium-strength long drink, is provided by

The Careful Man's Peachy Punch

5 bottles medium-dry white wine
4 bottles champagne cider (dry if possible)
2 bottles British peach wine
1 bottle vodka
2 lb. fresh peaches (more if possible,
and tinned if really necessary)
Ice cubes

Stone, cut up and soak the peaches as above. Put the cider in the refrigerator for a couple of hours beforehand. When the time comes, mix in the white wine, the peach wine and the vodka. Fill your jug, add ice, stir and pour, adding the chilled cider to each glass in the proportion of two from the jug to one from the bottle. Serve immediately.

Notes. (i) This will give you about sixty generous glasses at an outlay of about 15p each. If you can undercut me with anything similar, as strong and non-poisonous, I shall be interested to hear from you.

(ii) These British fruit wines are fortified up to a strength approaching that of sherry or vermouth – and sell at about 70p a bottle, which makes them, strength against price, an excellent buy. One would not perhaps want to drink more than, even as much as, one glass straight, but they are satisfactory in combination, as here. Besides peach there are apricot, red-currant, damson and cherry versions, so that even quite stupid and unimaginative careful men will not find much difficulty in improvising variations on the theme I have provided.

Jo Bartley's Christmas Punch

3 bottles dry or medium-dry white wine
2 bottles gin
1 bottle brandy
1 bottle sherry
1 bottle dry vermouth
5 quarts medium-sweet cider
Ice cubes

(If you feel like throwing in the unfinished drinks from last night, nobody will notice.) Mix everything together and serve from jugs that have some ice in them. Remember G.P. 4 and cut all the corners you can: Spanish wine, cocktail gin, non-cognac (but *not* non-French) brandy, British sherry and British vermouth; the cider will cover them and blend them into a new and splendid whole. Despite the potency that lurks behind its seeming mildness, I have never known anybody to suffer while or after drinking it.

I have named it after its creator, the scholar, wit and dear friend of mine who died in 1967.

Paul Fussell's Milk Punch

1 part brandy
1 part bourbon whiskey
4 parts fresh milk
Nutmeg
Frozen milk cubes

The previous evening (this is the hardest part) put milk instead of water into enough ice-trays in your refrigerator. On the day, mix the fresh milk and the spirits thoroughly together—in an electric blender, the deviser of the recipe says, and by all means do that if there is one lying about and not wanted by someone else and clean and with no bits missing and in working order. For me, stirring in a jug will do just as well. Pour into biggish glasses, drop in milk cubes, dust with nutmeg and serve.

This punch is to be drunk immediately on rising, in lieu of eating breakfast. It is an excellent heartener and sustainer at the outset of a hard day: not only before an air trip or an interview, but when you have in prospect one of those gruelling nominal festivities like Christmas morning, the wedding of an old friend of your wife's or taking the family over to Gran's for Sunday dinner.

Note. Do not, of course, use an expensive bourbon or a brandy that is anything more than just French. And taste each bottle of milk before pouring it in. There is a risk that sour-milk punch would not be as good.

Reginald Bosanquet's Golden Elixir

Champagne
Fresh peaches

The proportion is three biggish or four smallish peaches to one bottle; it is not critical. Put the stoned fruit through an electric blender—I hate the things, but I cannot think of a manual method that will do the job effectively. Pour the chilled champagne into wine glasses and top up with the strained peach-juice. 'The best drink in the world', says its creator with conviction. Very good, to be sure—and *healthy*.

Jittersauce

1 part Scotch
1 part gin
2 parts champagne
Ice cubes

Mix the Scotch and the gin, add ice, stir, pour champagne on top. This smooth-tasting drink, Robert Conquest tells me, was popular in some circles at Oxford in the late Thirties. It is a translation into action of the words of Cab Calloway, who at that time was in the habit of singing:

> If you want to be a jitterbug,
> First thing you do is git a mug;
> Pour whisky, gin and wine within,
> And then begin.

But try not to go on too long.

Evelyn Waugh's Noonday Reviver

1 hefty shot gin
1 (½-pint) bottle Guinness
Ginger beer

Put the gin and Guinness into a pint silver tankard and fill to the brim with ginger beer. I cannot vouch for the authenticity of the attribution, which I heard in talk, but the mixture will certainly revive you, or something. I should think two doses is the limit.

Woodrow Wyatt's Instant
Whiskey Collins

As much bourbon whiskey as you fancy
½ standard split-size bitter lemon drink
1 maraschino cherry
Ice cubes

You can work this one out for yourself. For once, you can
use rye or Irish whiskey or Scotch whisky* if you feel like it.
Whatever the purists may say, this is a good drink; it pays
to remember

   🐟G.P. 7: *Never despise a drink because it is easy to
make and/or uses commercial mixes. Unquestioning
devotion to authenticity is, in any department of life, a
mark of the naïve — or worse.*

The Bloody Mary

½ bottle vodka
2 pints tomato juice
2 tablespoons tomato ketchup
4 tablespoons lemon juice
4 tablespoons orange juice
1 tablespoon (at least) Worcester sauce
1 level teaspoon celery salt
Ice cubes

You will want to make up a lot of this before the party
starts, or before the last breakfasters have finished. Put
into some smallish container the vodka, ketchup, sauce and
celery salt. Stir furiously until the ketchup is fully emulsified

* Fact for the factually-minded: only Scotch may legally be spelt without
the 'e'.

and the lumps in the celery salt broken up. (The ketchup is the secret of the whole thing: I am not at all clear on what it does, but it does something considerable.) Mix the tomato juice and (strained) fruit juices into your usual jug, stir in the vodka-ketchup-sauce-salt mixture, add ice, stir again and serve in wine glasses or the equivalent; as with the Dry Martini, the bottom half of a too-large drink is warm when you get to it.

This delicious and sustaining potion is often thought to relieve hangovers, and certainly it will make you drunk again if you drink enough of it, but there is hardly anything distinctive about that. Some would argue that the tomato juice is food smuggled into a stomach that would shrink from it unsoftened with alcohol, to which one might reply that there are more digestible alternatives; further, that those whose stomachs are in fair shape, probably the majority, are having their appetites for lunch spoiled to no end. And yet, on the principle—very nearly worth erecting into a G.P.—that in all alcoholic matters subjectivism plays a big part, a lot of people will feel better after one or two Bloody Marys simply because they expect to.

La Tequila con Sangrita

*¼ pint plus (i.e. equal to the mixture
that follows) tequila
¼ pint tomato juice
1 tablespoon fresh lime juice (or 2
tablespoons fresh lemon juice)
½ teaspoon tabasco
1 small pinch cayenne pepper*

An exotic short-long drink to round off this section. I have never seen it served outside Mexico, though since drinking a good deal of it there I may not have looked very hard, I admit. Tequila is distilled from the juice of a cactus, and tastes like it, too. 'Sangrita' means 'little blood' or 'blood-ikins' (and 'con' means 'with', if you must know). The drink is a sort of Bloody Maria, very hot, and unique in being kept in two halves: the tomato concoction and the tequila do not meet until they arrive to start a joint operation on your stomach. Each partaker gets a small glass of neat, unchilled tequila and a twin glass of the stirred, also un-chilled red stuff, and sips at each in alternation.

I have had to specify $\frac{1}{4}$ pint because any smaller quantity makes the measurement of the other ingredients difficult; I am not suggesting that this is one round for one chap. The formula will serve three or so. You will find it a splen-did pick-me-up, and throw-me-down, and jump-on-me. Strongly disrecommended for mornings after.

HOT DRINKS

There is not much to be said in general about these either. They will warm you up, and they will make you drunk if you drink enough of them. Remember that their alcohol will affect you sooner than if you drank the same drink cold, chilled, iced. In those conditions the stomach must warm the stuff up to body temperature before absorption can take place; taken hot, it will start getting to you (or your girl-friend) at once. Ingredients, proportions and so on are not much more critical than with cold punches, as can be seen from this recipe for a

Generic Hot Punch

A lot of cheap red wine and/or cheap port-type wine

41

> *A glass or two or more of cheap (but French)*
> *brandy*
> *Some oranges and lemons*
> *Sugar*
> *Spices—cinnamon, nutmeg, cloves, etc.*
> *Water*

Put the sliced fruit into a saucepan (preferably one with a pouring beak), add and mix the wine and brandy and put on a slow gas. Stir in powdered spices if you feel like it, though about as much as these do in my experience is contribute a sediment. As the mixture warms, stir in castor sugar. Here you must use your judgment and keep tasting the result, which you will enjoy doing unless you are the wrong person to be giving the party.

Put a kettle on, get ready some expendable wine glasses or any sizeable glasses with a handle or, if you have them, those tumblers that fit inside raffia holders, and stand a dessertspoon in each. The moment the mixture in the saucepan has started to smoke, pour it into a pitcher (a stout enough one not to crack) and at once fill each glass half full. Add half as much boiling water to each drink, so that glasses are now threequarters full. The presence of the spoon will prevent the glasses cracking very nearly but not absolutely always; hence the 'expendable' proviso. Remove spoons and serve, bearing in mind that they should go back in momentarily whenever you top up drinks that are more than half drunk. Keep the remains in the saucepan on the stove, perhaps on an asbestos mat if you can handle the bloody things, remembering that as soon as the mixture starts to bubble, even slightly, you are boiling off alcohol.

Notes. (i) As always, 'cheap' wine, etc., does not mean any old plonk. Steer clear of Moroccan claret, Venezuelan tawny-port-style and such dubieties. As always, consult your wine merchant. On the other hand, never use good wine or real (Portuguese) port for a hot brew. They will be utterly wasted in that state. On yet another hand, if you ever find yourself saddled with a batch of non-lethal but unpalatable red wine, keep it by you for use in a hot punch, where its unpalatability will disappear.

(ii) Pundits will try to get you on to the fearful chore of roasting in the oven an orange stuck with real cloves, rubbing lemon rind off on lumps of sugar and all that. Pay no attention.

If, however, you want to offer something a little more than run-of-the-mill—and also rather less trouble—try

Portuguese Hot Punch

Bittall
Water

Proceed as above where appropriate, keeping the proportions of two wine and one hot water. The orange flavour of the Bittall comes through, rendering unnecessary any antics with fruit and the rest. You may need to stir in a little sugar, but I doubt it. I heartily recommend this simple drink.

The Polish Bison

1 generous teaspoon Bovril
1 (adjustable) tot vodka
Water
A squeeze of lemon juice (optional)
A shake of pepper

Make the Bovril as if you were merely making Bovril and stir the other stuff in. Named in salute to the nation that makes the best vodka, but its product will be wasted in this mixture: use a British version. This is a very cheering concoction, especially in cold and/or hungover conditions.

Hot Buttered Rum

Rum (any sort, but an expensive sort will be wasted)
Maple syrup
Butter
Water
Cinnamon

Put a generous tot of rum and a teaspoonful of maple syrup (or sugar syrup) in a mug, fill with hot water and stir till blended. Drop in a small knob of butter and dust with cinnamon. Not my discovery, but less well known, as warmer and nightcap, than it should be.

David Embury disagrees. He admits a version into his book for completeness' sake, but concludes sternly: 'How anyone can possibly consume [it] for pleasure is utterly beyond me … I believe that the drinking of Hot Buttered Rum should be permitted only in the Northwest Passage, and, even there, only by highly imaginative and over-enthusiastic novelists.' Dear dear.

Serbian Tea

Slivovitz (plum brandy)
Honey (the runny sort)

Heat the slivovitz in a saucepan and stir in honey to taste. Serve in small mugs. Much esteemed in the Balkans as a cold-cure. It does seem to help, but, in the words of one user, 'after a pint or so you can feel the lining of your stomach wearing thin.' So watch it.

Woe unto them that rise up early in the morning, that they may follow strong drink. —ISAIAH

He is not deserving the name of Englishman who speaketh against ale, that is, good ale. —GEORGE BORROW

ALFRED, LORD TENNYSON, Poet Laureate, on the occasion of his visit to the International Exhibition, 1862, having written an ode to be sung by a choir of four thousand at its opening: 'Is there anywhere in this damned place where we can get a decent bottle of Bass?'

What two ideas are more inseparable than Beer and Britannia? —SYDNEY SMITH

'I rather like bad wine,' said Mr Mountchesney; 'one gets so bored with good wine.' —BENJAMIN DISRAELI

There is nothing which has yet been contrived by man by which so much happiness is produced as by a good tavern or inn. —SAMUEL JOHNSON

'Champagne certainly gives one werry gentlemanly ideas, but for a continuance, I don't know but I should prefer mild hale.' —ROBERT SMITH SURTEES

Tools of the Trade

The aim here is to keep everything as simple as possible. Resist being led astray by any Compleat Barman's Presentation Wherewithal, which will be incompleat and largely unnecessary and badly designed, and accumulate your equipment only after personal inspection and careful thought. If you can rely on yourself not to be carried away, and I am far from sure I can rely on me when I have money to burn, you may visit the relevant departments of your local emporium. First as to your essential

BAR KIT

1. A refrigerator. All to yourself, I mean. There is really no way round this. Wives and such are constantly filling up any refrigerator they have a claim on, even its ice-compartment, with irrelevant rubbish like food. Get one of your own and have it fitted with racks the thickness of a bottle apart. This is not expensive and, adapted on these lines, even a small refrigerator will hold a lot of bottles and tins in an easy-to-get-at way. Use rubber or rubberoid ice-trays. The metal and the plastic ones have a longer life, but it is hell getting out the three or four cubes that are often all you need at a time; no problem with the rubber version.

2. A measuring-jug. The 1 pint/20 fl. oz. size is best.

3. A mixing-jug. This should be of glass, tall and narrow, with a lipped beak to hold in the ice when pouring. But check that it holds enough, not less than a quart. With a party of any size you will, when making a martini, say, want to use a bottle of spirits at a time and still leave plenty of room for ice and enthusiastic stirring.

4. An ice-container. With a Thermos lining and room for 30 or 40 cubes.

5. A bar spoon, i.e. with a long shank and a tiny bowl.

6. A lemon-squeezer. This should be of the acoustic sort, i.e. non-electrical, manual, and so always in working order. Plastic is better than glass, because the flutes on the central dome are usually sharper.

7. A strainer.

8. A really very sharp knife. (If you want to finish the evening with your usual number of fingers, do any cutting-up, peel-slicing and the like before you have had more than a couple of drinks, preferably before your first.)

9. A corkscrew. Go for the butterfly type or the sort that involves turning instead of pulling.

10. A crown-cork opener.

That is the lot. Keep them in a place only you have the key to, or they will not be there when you want them, I can assure you. (Locking up your refrigerator calls for some ingenuity, but good luck if you can get it fitted with a padlock.) Similarly, it will save you time in the end, as well as earning you domestic popularity, to do your own washing-up.

Half the point of the above list is what it leaves out. The most important and controversial of your non-needs is a cocktail-shaker. With all respect to James Bond, a martini should be stirred, not shaken. The case is a little different with drinks that include the heavier fruit-juices and liqueurs, but I have always found that an extra minute's stirring does the trick well enough. The only mixture that does genuinely need shaking is one containing eggs, and if that is your sort of thing, then clear off and buy yourself a shaker any time you fancy. The trouble with the things is that they are messy pourers and, much more important, they are far too small, holding half a dozen drinks at the outside. A shaker about the size of a hatbox might be worth pondering, but I have never seen or heard of such.

An electric blender is also unnecessary, though by all means use one if you are quite confident of not having to clean it afterwards. Those little battery-powered whirlers are fun to play with, but in my experience they do nothing that a vigorously rotated spoon will not do.

Ice-tongs have become acceptably replaced by the human hand. Thanks to the ring-and-tab arrangement, beer-tin openers are no longer required, and, thanks to the innovation of the screw cap, item 10 of the kit will be droppable any day.

The same policy of sticking to essentials has been followed in selecting your

GLASSES

1. A wine glass holding about eight ounces when full, though it's a sensible general rule not to fill it more than about two-thirds of the way up. (Same goes for sherry, port, etc.) It will do for all wines, including champagne. The only essentials are that the bowl should be the right shape to be cupped in the palm for warming a chilly red wine, and that there should be some sort of stem to prevent your fingers warming a white wine.

Those hock and moselle glasses with the brown and

green stems respectively are pretty and practical enough, but they break easily, and you may earn cries of horror and contempt if you try to serve anything but hock or moselle in them, so they are an extra, or an extravagance.

A third characteristic of the decent wine glass is one it shares with all other decent glasses: the part containing the drink, indeed the whole thing in the case of tumblers, etc., *must* be of plain glass so that you can see and appreciate the colour of the wine (though a light floral or similar pattern on a basic plain-glass ground is acceptable).

There are plenty of coloured drinking glasses about, and not quite all of them are horrible to look at, but the exceptions belong on your display shelf, not on your table. If somebody you are really very anxious to outdo should ever try to give you black burgundy, or bottle-green beer, ask politely if you can have it out of a white plastic tooth-mug instead, explaining that that at least allows you to see the true colour of the drink from above.

2. A sherry glass. This, filled to the brim, should hold about six ounces. It should have a stem to avoid hand-heating, like the wine glass, but that stem need only be long enough to be held comfortably between thumb and forefinger. The shape is up to you. I favour a sort of small wine glass with a U-shaped bowl. In this you can, with perfect propriety, serve not only sherry, but port, vermouth, liqueurs and brandy. Yes, brandy. If you notice any foreheads beginning to pucker at this, say you have always thought the traditional brandy snifter looked frightfully pompous and silly, and add carelessly that only inferior brandies are worth sniffing anyway. If you object that the amount of liqueur you feel like dispensing to your guests appears rather mean in a six-ounce glass, then you are just a mean sod.

3. An Old-Fashioned glass. In other words, a short

broad tumbler holding about eight ounces when full. The point of it is not just that it looks pretty—though it does, very—but that in it you can get a lot of ice cubes into a short drink without piling them up above the surface and so numbing the drinker's nose. It is an ideal vessel not only for the Old-Fashioned cocktail but for anything drunk on the rocks: spirits, vermouths, wine apéritifs like Dubonnet, Punt e Mes, etc.

4. A Highball or Collins glass. In other words, a tall thin tumbler holding 11 or 12 ounces or something over half a pint. This will do for all long drinks from gin and tonic onwards. You can serve beer in it if pushed, but at the cost of hand-heating, and on this and other grounds I favour

5. A beer glass. The familiar pub tankard with handle. The half-pint size is the more generally useful, but a few pint ones will come in handy, not only for pints, but for Pimm's* (the presence of ice and all that vegetation makes the half-pint Pimm's a rather short-weight affair) and long drinks that froth up a lot, like Black Velvet. (It goes against the grain to have to spell out such common knowledge in a treatise on the present level, but this 'sour and invigorating draught', as Evelyn Waugh called it, consists of equal parts of chilled Guinness and chilled champagne, with the latter put in first. Try it with a sweeter stout if the champagne, or your stomach, is on the acid side.) These glasses are not always easy to come by. Inquire from your wine merchant or at your off-licence.

No, Sir, claret is the liquor for boys; port for men; but he who aspires to be a hero [smiling] must drink brandy ... Brandy will do soonest for a man what drinking *can* do for him. —SAMUEL JOHNSON

* Few such things are more worth the trouble than adding a little cucumber juice and lemon juice to each portion of Pimm's.

The Store Cupboard

... is not the same place as the cellar or the larder or wherever you keep your stock for daily use. In other words, I am not insulting your (in many respects) considerable intelligence by letting you know that to lay in some gin, wine, beer, etc., is a good idea if you want to get a spot of drinking done; I am taking up an earlier point of mine about the relatively uncommon liquors called for in some cocktail and other recipes, and will go on to suggest a basic set that will enable you to try your hand at some of the more out-of-the-way mixtures. A small basic set: to be in a position to make every drink in David Embury's book, for instance, would call for a store cupboard, or room, holding something like four hundred different bottles, not to speak of a small greengrocer-fruiterer's shop and a miniature dairy.

The liquors referred to are mostly liqueurs. (I know the latter are primarily intended to be drunk separately; I know too how it feels next day to have drunk a lot of one or more of them separately – see The Hangover.) A general word on these fatal Cleopatras of the world of booze comes in quite handily here. They are not really worth individual notice, except for *kitró*, little known and so justifying a brief digression. *Kitró* is little known because you have to go to the Greek island of Naxos to get it – the neighbouring island of Ios produces another and slightly less nectarean version. They do not export it even to the Greek mainland; at any rate, I have never found it there after plenty of looking. It is based on the lemon, but seemingly on the rind as well as the juice, hence its peculiar tang. Should you find yourself in Athens, you seriously should make the trip to Naxos, or Ios, and come away with as many bottles as you can carry. They are nice islands anyhow, even when not seen through a *kitró*-haze.

To resume, then: a liqueur can be defined as a strong drink with a fruity or herbal flavour. There are two main families: a thinner kind made by distilling the fermented juices of fruits other than the grape, such as pears, strawberries, apples, plums, and a thicker kind made by mingling brandy, sugar, and fruit juice or herbal infusions. The first kind is little used in mixed drinks and need not concern us here. The second kind subdivides, the largest group consisting of liqueurs with an orange flavour. These may be dark in colour—Curaçao, Grand Marnier, Van der Hum: the last is flavoured with a fruit that is not exactly an orange, but I have shoved it in here—or white, like Cointreau and Triple Sec. (The latter name, for one of the sweetest drinks ever made, must be a joke.) All have their own individual flavour, but the difference will hardly show in a mixture, especially when lemon juice is also present, as it often is; so pick from this group the one you like best straight and use it whenever any of them comes up in a recipe. Adopt the same principle with the cherry group—Maraschino, Cherry Heering and the Dutch version made by Bols.

There are other necessary liqueurs which are not interchangeable, which I include below, together with one or two miscellaneous items. Your store cupboard, then, should contain:

1. An orange liqueur.
2. A cherry liqueur.

L'absinthe est interdit

3. Bénédictine—which needs no introduction.

4. Crème de Menthe—ditto. Pundits say the white sort is better than the green, but I cannot tell the difference in flavour, and the green is much prettier, and you can never find the white anyway.

5. Crème de Cacao. A very thick drink supposedly tasting of cocoa. Gives mixtures an individual twist, but not recommended for drinking straight. The least indispensable on this list.

6. A pseudo-absinthe such as Pernod or Ricard. True absinthe (the name is from a Greek word meaning 'undrinkable') has been illegal in most places for a long time. It is, or was, flavoured with the herb wormwood, which, as the French authorities noticed after years of using absinthe in their army to combat fever, 'acts powerfully on the nerve-centres, and causes delirium and hallucinations, followed in some cases by idiocy' (*Encyclopedia Britannica*). The perfectly wholesome successors to absinthe are flavoured with anis, or aniseed. The result always reminds me, not unpleasantly, of those paregoric cough-sweets children ate before the war, and I see that paregoric does contain aniseed, but throws in opium, camphor and benzoic acid as well, so I am probably just being nostalgic. Anyway, when recipes call for absinthe, as they can still do if their compilers and revisers have been too ignorant or lazy to make the change, use Pernod or Ricard instead.

Incidentally, what happened about vermouth, which is or was also flavoured with wormwood?—'vermouth' being a French or German attempt to say 'wormwood'. Could the idiocy, or bloody foolishness, which comes to afflict the multi-martini-man be the result of the wormwood in the vermouth? No. It is the alcohol, you see. (And I suspect it was the alcohol in the absinthe, too, that caused the trouble all along, when the stuff was taken to excess.)

7. A bottle of orange bitters, a decent-sized one. Avoid the little shakers got up to look like the Angostura article.

8. A bottle of grenadine. A non-alcoholic, sweetened sort of pomegranate juice, nice to look at, odd in flavour — I am never sure whether I like it or not. But quite a few recipes include it.

9. A bottle of sugar syrup, a preparation continually called for in mixed-drink books. To have a supply of it will save you a lot of time when making up, for instance, my Old-Fashioned and Normandy recipes. Concoct it yourself by the following simple method:

Down a stiff drink and keep another by you to see you through the ordeal. Put a pound of castor or cube sugar in a saucepan with half a pint of water and bring the dissolving mixture to the boil. Keep it there for five minutes. Let it cool and pour into an old (clean) spirits bottle. *The Constance Spry Cookery Book* recommends adding a teaspoon of liquid glucose to the sugar and water, as a guard against later crystallization.

Remember you are dealing with one of the stickiest substances known, so select with forethought the surface where you will do the pouring, and cover it with a month's old newspapers. For the same reason, bind some flannel or something round your bottle to absorb stray dribbles from its mouth — so see that its neck is long enough — or make a collar for it from one of those plastic sponges that harden when dry.

Your bottleful will last for months, and you will have been constantly patting yourself on the back for your wisdom and far-sightedness.

Slimmers can save both time and weight by using a liquid artificial sweetener and establishing the quantities needed by trial and error. There is a flavour problem here, but remember that the sweetener will generally be sweetening a mixture of flavours much more powerful on the palate than tea or coffee. Up to you.

Note. I have assumed you realize that the above are not the only extras you need to supplement your fundamental gin, vodka, whisky, rum, brandy, etc. You will also, of course, have to have French and Italian vermouths, Campari, Angostura bitters, tonic water and all that lot. But I take these to form part of your daily stock.

Freedom and Whisky gang thegither! —ROBERT BURNS

Wine snob —a man or woman who drinks the label and the price. —OLOF WIJK

Porter. ... drink, sir, is a great provoker of three things.
Macduff. What three things does drink especially provoke?
Porter. Marry, sir, nose-painting, sleep, and urine. Lechery, sir, it provokes, and unprovokes: it provokes the desire, but it takes away the performance: Therefore much drink may be said to be an equivocator with lechery; it makes him, and it mars him; it sets him on, and it takes him off; it persuades him, and disheartens him; makes him stand to, and not stand to: in conclusion, equivocates him in a sleep, and, giving him the lie, leaves him.

WILLIAM SHAKESPEARE, *Macbeth*

They who drink beer will think beer. —WASHINGTON IRVING

First Thoughts on Wine

Deep colour and big shaggy nose. Rather a jumbly, untidy sort of wine, with fruitiness shooting off one way, firmness another and body pushing about underneath. It will be as comfortable and as comforting as the 1961 Nuits-St-Georges once it has pulled its ends in and settled down.

That genuine extract from a wine journal is the sort of thing that gets the stuff a bad name with a lot of people who would enjoy wine if they could face trying it seriously. Let it be said at once that talking about big shaggy noses and so forth receives a deeper and more educated contempt from real wine-drinkers than from the average man in the pub. But, before I get to a more positive approach, let me describe, in careful stages, not what you should do when serving wine to your guests, but what you nearly always do (if you are anything like me):

　1. Realize that They will be arriving in less than an hour and you have done damn-all about it.
　2. Realize, on your way to the cellar or wherever you keep the stuff, that the red wine to go with the roast beef will be

nowhere near the required room temperature if left to warm up unassisted.

3. Realize, on reaching the stuff, that it has not had time to 'settle' after being delivered, and that you should have realized six weeks—or, if you had wanted to give Them a treat, ten years—ago exactly what wine you were going to need tonight.

4. Decide that They can bloody well take what They are given, grab some bottles and take them to the kitchen.

5. Take the foil off the necks of the bottles. (Now that the bottlers have mostly decided they can cut costs by leaving the lead out of this, your present task is like removing nail-polish with a fish-knife.)

6. Look for the corkscrew.

7. Having (we will assume) found the corkscrew, unscrew the cork that somebody has left screwed on it and open the bottles.

8. Find something to take the gunk or crap off the bottle-necks and take it off.

9. Decide that, while any fool can tell when wine is cold, and nearly any fool knows nowadays that a red wine is not supposed to be cold, hardly anyone knows a decent glass of it from a bad one, and stick the bottles in a saucepan of warm water.

10. Spend parts of the next hour-and-a-half wondering whether old Shagbag, who is reputed to know one wine from another, will denounce you for boiling out whatever quality tonight's stuff might have had, or will suffer in silence. Also wonder whether the others will think 1971 a rather insultingly recent year for a Médoc, whether to get up another bottle on the off-chance that They can force down what you have 'prepared' for the table, whether to boil that too or to bank on Their being too drunk to notice or too polite to mention its coldness, and kindred questions.

11. Do not enjoy the wine much yourself when you come to drink it.

Now let me contrast the procedure when serving beer:

1. Do nothing at all before you get to table, beyond ensuring you have enough.

2. At table, inquire, 'Anyone not for beer?'

3. Subtract the number so signifying from the total sitting down.

4. From larder or refrigerator bring one tin of beer for each person concerned, tear off the tabs and start pouring, in the total certainty that the stuff will be all right.

5. Say, 'If anyone wants any more he's only got to shout.'

Streamlined version of the above:

1. Five minutes before everybody goes 'in', put one tin of beer at each place.

2. Let the sods open and pour themselves.

The point is that wine is *a lot of trouble*, requiring energy and forethought. I would agree without hesitation that (if the comparison can properly be made at all) the best wine is much better than the best beer, though many would not, at least in private, and many more will bless you under their breath for giving them a decent Worthington or Double Diamond instead of what they too often get, Algerian red ink under a French label. And this is the other half of the wine/beer comparison: a lot of beer is probably better than a lot of wine, in this country at any rate.

Those who take this view are in a difficult position. The pro-wine pressure on everybody who can afford to drink at all is immense and still growing. To offer your guests beer instead of wine (unless you are serving a curry, a Scandinavian cold table, eggs and bacon, etc.) is to fly in the face of trend as well as of established custom. It looks—and in some cases it no doubt is—neglectful and mean. Worse, it may seem affected, bogusly no-nonsensical, as who should say, 'Tek thi ale and be glad on it, lad; it wor good enough for mi dad home from pit and mi mam home from mill' — an attitude common enough among wealthy socialists, but hardly the thing for you and me. Lastly, for every secret beer-drinker you may please by your policy, you will displease at least one open wine-drinker. The latter may not be able to tell a Chablis from a Château d'Yquem, be entirely motivated by snobbery, but, under that old basic rule, if he thinks he likes wine, he likes wine. What is to be done?

I said right at the beginning that you cannot give your guests good drinks without taking a lot of trouble, and even though the trouble you have to take about wine is extra troublesome, and differs from the kind of trouble you take with (say) a dry martini, in that sufficient trouble over a dry martini guarantees a good dry martini, whereas a hell of a lot of trouble over wine is in itself no such guarantee — even so, we have to soldier on with the stuff, relieving our feelings every now and then with such things as the not very balanced or temperate outburst near the start of this section. I have therefore devised

The Wine-Resenter's Short Handy Guide

1. Keep saying to yourself (what is true) that really good and properly served clarets and red burgundies are the best drinks yet devised by man. (I have admittedly never had the chance of tasting, among other things, kumiss, the drink made by the nomadic Tatars out of fermented mares' or camels' milk, but I doubt if it is even as good, let alone better.)

2. Always drink wine, except with curry and so on, when

you eat out in restaurants and especially at your friends' houses. You may learn something: see (4) below.

3. At least serve *white* wine at home whenever the food permits. It needs only to be served cold, though not too cold (an hour in the refrigerator is about right), and you are exempted from those horrible moments of discovering that you ought to have opened it three hours earlier. My advice would be to stick to hocks and moselles, which everybody likes, and avoid white burgundies, which some people prefer to almost anything, but which others will find too dry, whatever the depth of their superstition about the okayness of dryness. 'Closely resembling a blend of cold chalk soup and alum cordial with an additive or two to bring it to the colour of children's pee' was how a character in a novel of mine described, perhaps opinionatedly, the generic white burgundy.

4. Get yourself a first-rate wine merchant. I do not just mean a reputable one who will invariably sell you wholesome drinks at not-excessive prices; they will all do this; I have never yet come across a disreputable wine merchant. What you want is a learned, experienced, energetic man who himself drinks not only good wine but a lot of wine, in other words a *first-rate* wine merchant. How you find him is another question. Go for a small or smallish firm, who have the chance of getting to know the individual customer and his tastes. Ask your friends. Grab a fellow wine-resenter and make a start on the classified directory.

5. Having found your man, trust him. Ask him for a decent drinkable red you will enjoy yourself and can offer to guests without shame. These days this will cost you £1 a bottle. Resign yourself to that. Also ask for a treat wine for anniversaries and when old Shagbag comes to dinner. This will cost £3 a bottle. Resign yourself to *that*. There are also, of course, wines at £2, and listen carefully to what your

chap says about them. Also take his advice on hocks and moselles, shutting your ears when he rhapsodizes about white burgundies.

6. Grit your teeth and do as much as you can bear of the let-it-settle, bring-it-up-ahead-of-time, open-it-well-before-drinking routine. It really will make a difference. But bear in mind

> 🪝 G.P. 8: *Careful preparation will render a poor wine just tolerable and a very nice wine excellent. Skimping it will diminish a pretty fair wine to all right and a superb wine to merely bloody good. That is about as much difference as it will make. Much more important is price, which is normally a very reliable indicator of quality. Nevertheless*

You will find that, when you are confident of serving something at least reasonably drinkable, you will be the more anxious to improve it by taking trouble beforehand.

7. Hit your wine merchant across the mouth when, innocently trying to put you on to a good thing, or what he sees as one, he recommends you to 'buy for laying down'. It is true that wine improves and increases in value with age, broadly speaking, and that you can save a lot of money (and worry) by seeing to it that the ageing takes place after, rather than before, you buy it. But 'Pay now, drink in 1984' strikes me—perhaps me more than most, but indubitably me—as a dreadfully depressing slogan. (It is this consideration, by the way, that hurls out of court any scheme for making your own beer, mead, elderflower wine, etc., though stand ready to drink *other people's* home-made brews like mad: they are often amazingly good. 'Cork tightly and keep for eighteen months' the books will gaily enjoin, when continuing in suspense for eighteen minutes is rather more than most respectable drink-men would be

justified to endure.) Fork out your £1-3 and look and feel pleasant. Life is too short.

8. Keep at hand a good supply of beer, stout and cider, not to speak of stronger waters, to console you when the whole business gets too much for you.

If all be true that I do think
There are five reasons we should drink;
Good wine – a friend – or being dry –
Or lest we should be by and by –
Or any other reason why.

HENRY ALDRICH (1648-1710)

Ale, man, ale's the stuff to drink
For fellows whom it hurts to think:
Look into the pewter pot
To see the world as the world's not.

A. E. HOUSMAN

If ever I marry a wife,
    I'll marry a landlord's daughter,
For then I may sit in the bar,
    And drink cold brandy and water.

CHARLES LAMB

I would to God that I were so much clay
    As I am blood, bone, matter, passion, feeling;
For then at least the past were past away,
    And for the future – but I write this reeling,
Having got drunk exceedingly today,
    So that I seem to stand upon the ceiling:
I say, the future is a serious matter;
But now, for God's sake, hock and soda-water!

LORD BYRON

Further Thoughts on Wine *

for the man whose curiosity on the subject has not been totally assuaged by the foregoing.

1. Make up your mind to drink wine *in quantity*. I am not exactly advising you to add three bottles of vintage claret to your normal daily intake, but even when drunk to excess, wine has less severe short-term and long-term effects on your condition than an excess of spirits or fortified wines (sherry, port). Unless you are uncontrollably rich, in which case you are probably not deigning to read this, try the cheap table wines from France, Spain, Portugal or Austria that are sold under brand names in every off-licence. They are carefully blended to ensure that their taste and general standard remain constant, and are an excellent basis from which to start your more ambitious forays into the vintages. Shop around until you find one you really go for, but carry on shopping around after that.

2. Also shop around under your wine merchant's auspices. Ask him to make up an assorted case for you—two bottles each of six different wines is better than one each of a

* This and the two following sections were compiled with the aid of my friend Christopher Leaver.

Six of one and half a dozen of the other

dozen—and tell him whether you prefer dry or sweet, light or heavy, cheap or not so cheap. Repeat the treatment *ad libitum.*

3. Join a wine club. There are plenty of these springing up; there might be one in your area; your wine merchant might be able to recommend one. You may even find a course on wine being given by your local night school, especially in London under the G.L.C.

4. On the principle of not barking yourself if you keep a dog, test out the wine waiter whenever you eat in a restaurant, as follows. If he wears a little silver badge in his lapel, he is a member of the Guild of Sommeliers (cellarmen), and you stand a chance. If, asked what he recommends, he shows no interest in what you are eating, or refers to a wine merely by its number on the list, consign him to hell either silently or aloud, according to taste. If, requested to fetch a Pommard 1966 domaine-bottled, he leans over to see where you are pointing and says, 'Ah yes, a bottle of Number 65—that is very good,' he is no less of a villain, for he has shown he does not even know his way round his cellar, let alone have any idea of what is good or not so good in it. If he passes so far, and if you are in a tolerant, unexacting frame of mind, you may let him guide you. But if he then brings you something that you think is either ordinary at a high price or nasty at any, tell him so and *make him sample it himself.* This will take him down a satisfying peg, however hotly he may protest on tasting that the wine is first-rate, and he might even—who knows?—try a little harder next time. If you want to cut out all fuss and argument, simply ask for a carafe of the house hock, claret or whatever. This, without necessarily being very good to drink, will always be good value, because the management must both keep its price down and see to it that it remains at a consistent not-bad level. And if, of course, you want

to put the wine waiter down, study the wine list long and carefully before handing it back with a smiling shake of the head and ordering your carafe: a hefty implication that either they have nothing up to the standard you and your guests expect, which is conceivable, or they are charging too much for their listed wines, which is quite likely.

5. Follow the advice of wine merchants, wine clubs, wine waiters, even wine journalists, but never forget that your own taste is the final judge. Like the solicitor who keeps his clientèle safely under sedation by the use of fanciful legal jargon—did you know that any fool can do his own conveyancing, i.e. legally transfer property between himself and another?—so the wine snob, the so-called expert and the jealous wine merchant (there are a few) will conspire to persuade you that the subject is too mysterious for the plain man to penetrate without continuous assistance. This is, to put it politely, disingenuous flummery. It is up to you to drink what you like and can afford. You would not let a tailor tell you that a pair of trousers finishing a couple of inches below the knee actually fitted you perfectly; so, with wine, do not be told what is correct or what you are sure to like or what suits you. Specifically:

(a) Drink any wine you like with any dish. You will, in practice, perhaps find that a heavy red burgundy drowns the taste of oysters (though my wife likes claret with them), or that a light flowery hock is overpowered by a steak *au poivre*. But what is wrong with red wine and chicken, a light claret accompanying a Dover sole? The no-reds-with-fish superstition is widespread and ingrained, so much so that, in the film of *From Russia, With Love*, James Bond was able to say, in jest but without further explanation, that he ought to have spotted one of the opposition when the man broke that 'rule' in the dining-car of the Orient Express. All he should reasonably have inferred was that the chap was rather independent-minded. I myself will happily drink red with any fish, and the fact that I will even more happily drink a hock, a moselle or an Alsatian wine with my fish stems from the other fact that I am particularly fond of hocks, moselles and Alsatian wines. The North of England couple I once read about who shared a bottle of crème de menthe (I hope it was a half-bottle) to go with their grilled turbot should be an inspiration, if not a literal example, to us all. Anyway, why not start by choosing a wine you know you like and then build your meal round it?

(b) Vintages—aargh! Most of the crap talked about wine centres on these. 'The older the better' is another popular pseudo-rule. It does apply up to a point to château-bottled clarets, especially those known as classed growths. This is a precise technical term, not a piece of wine-snobs' jargon, but I cannot expound it here; consult your wine merchant or wine encyclopedia. There are rich men who will drink nothing but old first-growth clarets to show their friends how well they know their wines (and how rich they are). These are likely to be wonderful wines, true, but such men are missing a lot—see below. And old wines as such are not necessarily good; they may well have gone off or always have been bad, whatever that bloody vintage chart or card may have said. Throw it away, or keep it in a drawer until you know the subject a bit and can pick up cheap the good wines of a 'bad' year.

6. A couple of warnings. Beware of curiously shaped or oddly-got-up bottles: you are likely to be paying for the parcel rather than what is wrapped up in it. I would not want to decry Mateus Rosé, a pleasant enough drink which has been many a youngster's introduction to wine, but its allure, and its price, owe a lot to the work of the glassmaker. Also, beware of those imitation champagnes called sparkling burgundies. They are forms of bottled death. (Leaver's

phrase and view; Amis is defiantly rather fond of red sparkling burgundy. He admits he has never found any food it can be drunk with, but a half-bottle of it makes a — shall we say? — interesting aperitif and, if you handle the situation properly, ordering it, let alone appearing to enjoy it, can be a splendid knock-down to any companion who fancies himself as a bit of an expert on wine. It is without doubt the most vulgar drink known to man.)

> A bumper of good liquor
> Will end a contest quicker
> Than justice, judge, or vicar.
> RICHARD BRINSLEY SHERIDAN

> The horse and mule live 30 years
> And nothing know of wines and beers.
> The goat and sheep at 20 die
> And never taste of Scotch or Rye.
> The cow drinks water by the ton
> And at 18 is mostly done.
> The dog at 15 cashes in
> Without the aid of rum and gin.
> The cat in milk and water soaks
> And then in 12 short years it croaks.
> The modest, sober, bone-dry hen
> Lay eggs for nogs, then dies at 10.
> All animals are strictly dry:
> They sinless live and swiftly die;
> But sinful, ginful, rum-soaked men
> Survive for three score years and ten.
> And some of them, a very few,
> Stay pickled till they're 92.

ANON, quoted in Arnold Silcock's *Verse and Worse*

Wine Shopper's Guide

In choosing your wine, whether from a supplier's price-list or in a restaurant, the obvious temptation is to go for a name you recognize. You would not recognize it unless it had a long reputation for quality; but such reputations set prices rising, and unfamiliar names may well bring you better value for money. As regards home drinking, faith in your wine merchant's recommendations will bring you that value and also provide you with interesting variety. In the restaurant, a good policy is to forget names, labels and vintages and go for a wine imported by a shipper whose wares you have enjoyed in the past. This brings up a general point of some importance.

Two bottles of a wine of the same year and from the same district will not necessarily taste the same. Soils can vary from one side of the road to the other; the vines on a southern slope will get more sun than those on a northern; M. Crapaud's processes may differ from M. Grenouille's. This becomes particularly noticeable in a large area like Beaune in Burgundy.* Shippers' methods differ too. One

* Point for pedants. The established rule is a capital for the place and a small letter for the wine, so you drink burgundy in Burgundy (if you have the luck), see that your champagne comes from one of the best spots in Champagne. This breaks down when we come to districts within a wine-producing

well-known firm matures its Meursault (a—usually—white burgundy from a sub-district within Beaune) in cask for three years before bottling; others bottle after two or even one. This is where your wine merchant comes in: he will know how individual shippers handle their wine, and will guide you to the one(s) who suit(s) your taste. (Shop salesmen are rarely much good for this kind of help, though their knowledge is, by and large, increasing.) Finally, have no fear of non-vintage 'house' *vins ordinaires* labelled simply Red Bordeaux (etc.). They are nearly always better than all right, and excellent value.

Now to the wines of individual regions.

1. BORDEAUX. Reds (clarets). Here you have a couple of hundred different names to cope with, if you feel you must cope. One you recognize does carry with it a sort of guarantee: nowadays, the well-known châteaux can, by blending, offer a vintage every year regardless, and are too careful of their reputation to produce any bad wine under their label. But, as suggested earlier, you will to some extent be paying for the name. For better value for money, look for wines from these three districts: Côtes de Bourg, Côtes de Blaye and Côtes de Fronsac. They will be of a recent year, but never mind: they mature fast. 75p to £1 retail.* You will almost certainly have to pay much more than that for something good under more familiar names like Médoc or St Emilion.

Whites—specifically sweet whites. These can be first-rate value. Non-vintage Sauternes and Barsacs at 80–90p are delicious with fruit (or cheese) and for lingering over at

region. I have yet to read of anybody calling for a nice médoc or knocking back a glass of pouilly fuissé.

*What with the floating of the pound, the coming of V.A.T., etc., drink prices are on the rise. All the ones I quote are approximate.

the end of a meal. If you have more to spend and fancy something really luscious and fruity, you can get château-bottled* wines like Château Climens or Château Rieussec for £1·50 or less.

2. BURGUNDY. Wines with Burgundian village names, such as Pommard, Gevrey-Chambertin, Chambolle Musigny or Vosne Romanée, are becoming dearer and dearer and less and less value for money. It is even hard to find genuine examples of them, unless they are bottled by a highly reputable shipper, by your own wine merchant, or, best of all, at the *domaine* – which is to burgundy as château is to Bordeaux wines. The better-known names, like Nuits St Georges, are starting to disappear from merchants' lists; supply cannot meet demand, prices have shot up, and the 'stretching' (=adulterating) of wines in the recent past has led to a virtual insistence on the growers' part that their product be bottled on the spot: more lowering of supply and increase in price. The answer is to look for less famous names, such as Givry, Fixin, Mercurey and Monthélie. These are ready to drink within four years of the vintage. In general, drink neither reds nor whites too old – ten years old is too old – and, as before, remember shippers' names.

Whatever I may have said elsewhere, the dry white wines of Burgundy are very good value, probably the best of their type in France. Go for Pouilly Fuissé, which can be drunk young at something under £1. Chablis, Meursault, Puligny Montrachet will cost you a little more.

2a. BEAUJOLAIS. (This is strictly a sub-region of Burgundy, but it is usually spoken and thought of as a region in its own right.) It was said, not very comfortably long ago, that the French and the British between them

---

* Bottled at the place of origin. A château in the wine sense is not literally a castle; it is much more likely to be a straggle of sheds.

drank every year five times the amount of beaujolais that Beaujolais annually produced. I believe, or perhaps merely hope, that since this became fairly common knowledge, and since the French had to get out of Algeria, we have returned to drinking real beaujolais. Anyway, what we now get under that name will cost about £1, and should be attacked in quantity, like beer, and, like beer, slightly chilled, and, like beer, as soon after bottling as you like—so, at any rate, with anything labelled just beaujolais or Beaujolais Villages. Moulin-à-Vent and Morgon need a couple of years in bottle. Fleurie, Brouilly and Chiroubles are good too.

Pink or rosé wines are sometimes looked down on as ladies' or non-drinkers' wines, but Beaujolais Rosé has more to it than most, being dry and—an oddity—servable either slightly chilled or at room temperature and with either hot or cold meals. One shipper claims you can drink it with curry, but I have not tested this. Good value at about 90p.

3. RHONE. The full, strong reds of these southern vineyards deserve to be better known. Everybody has heard of Châteauneuf du Pape (the white is good, too), but less famous names can be better value: Lirac, St Joseph, Crozes-Hermitage, Cornas, Gigondas. Being comparatively obscure, they are not shipped for chain distribution and hence there is no need to stretch them. They are well worth buying English-bottled whenever they can be found on a wine merchant's list, but you should not go above £1 or so.

With an exception or two, the whites are not really up to much. Tavel Rosé from the Rhône is always considered one of the best French rosés, but I find it rather dull. You may like it, though.

4. LOIRE. As the Rhône produces some of the best value in French reds, so the Loire for dry whites, but these are nearly always better when French-bottled.

Muscadet, Touraine Blanc and Vouvray are each about £1. Sancerre and Pouilly Fumé are better and pricier. All are excellent with sea-food or as an apéritif.

Reds: Chinon and St Nicholas de Bourgeuil really are fruity, often with a raspberryish flavour, but will run you into money: £1·50 or more. Rosé: Anjou Rosé, medium sweet. Sweet dessert white: Quarts de Chaume. Sparkling: Saumur, made in the champagne manner, but cheaper, and far from being bottled death. Good for summer mornings, weddings, etc.

5. ALSACE. Until recently, the Alsace whites (no reds are made) were very good value for money, but they have become popular and dearer. Each is named after the type of grape it is made from. Sylvaner and Riesling are good and not expensive at 90p or so. Traminer and Gewurtztraminer will take you up to £1·50, but have an extraordinary herby flavour all their own. Tokay d'Alsace is a toothsome dry wine at £1·25 or so. I like them all, but my favourite is Muscat, made, clearly enough, from the muscatel grape but without a trace of sweetness; about £1·25. Do try it—but leave some for me.

6. CHAMPAGNE. Any wine from France under this name will be good. By and large, you need not pay the extra 50p or so for vintage champagne. Bollinger N.V., one of the driest of all, is often as good as other people's vintage quality. Some pink champagne is made, but if you are with somebody who knows about these things, have a counter-attack ready when you order it. Some sweet champagne is made, and very horrible it is.

7. GERMAN WINES. These divide broadly into moselles or mosels, from the valley of the river of that name, and hocks or Rhine wines, from the valley of the guess-which. All, or all you will ever see unless you go there, are white. Generally, and in the cheaper range especially, moselles

are drier and thinner than hocks, which are more varied. At under £1, look for such moselles as Piesporter and Zeltinger, and, at perhaps a little more, for Bernkasteler — Deinhard's Bernkasteler 'Green Label' is splendid value. With hocks, start with the wines of Niersteiner, find one you like, note the shipper and proceed from there.

Whatever the men in the know may say, a German wine label is a fearful thing to decipher. It tells you (starting at the top of the bottle) the vintage, the name of the village, the vineyard, the type of grape — moselles are always made from the riesling type, and in their case this information is usually omitted, which makes things even more straightforward — the state of maturity of the grape when picked, in effect whether or not the wine was German-bottled, and the name of the grower or shipper. All very conscientious, but more than I want to know. However: note, as always, the shipper's name, and you can learn something from the state-of-maturity bit, the word invariably ending in -lese. *Spaetlese*, or 'late picked', means a higher quality and often a good buy. *Beerenauslese* and *Trockenbeerenauslese* signify respectively selected grapes and selected overripe grapes, and produce the great sweet wines of Germany. I have never found one of these to beat a Château d'Yquem, the finest and most expensive of the Sauternes, but then I have never drunk a 1959 *Trockenbeerenauslese*. You can, if you can find one and can lay out £20 *a bottle*.

There are sparkling hocks and moselles. I can hear Leaver muttering about bottled death, and some people find them a little headachy, but I never have. They are considerably cheaper than champagne, can usually be passed off as it with the aid of a napkin round the bottle (a good tip for the mean man), and will certainly enliven a wine punch.

8. OTHERS. In general, these are best approached under merchants' advice or via your off-licence as described in the first paragraph of my Further Thoughts on Wine, but here are a few notes.

Italy. Remember that chianti is not the only Italian wine; some people will find some of the reds a little heavy (cut them with Pellegrino mineral water). Barolo is a good solid red, and Soave a nice lightish white.

Spain. Rioja is usually spoken of as the best Spanish red. Avoid all sweet whites, and according to some (me included) the dry whites are not very nice either.

Portugal. Dão, both red and white. Mateus Rosé for student-age types.

Switzerland. If you are flush, try the full but soft red Dôle and the light white wines of Neuchâtel and Fendant.

Algeria. There are plenty of sound full-blooded reds at about 75p.

Yugoslavia. The Lutomer wines are usually good value and quite cheap.

Hungary. Bull's Blood is a fine strong red. You must try Tokay, the famous sweet desert and after-dinner wine.

FINAL NOTE

If you can afford the initial outlay (about £150 for something drinkable, £190 for something really good), buy a hogshead and bottle it yourself. You will end up with something like 300 bottles and save about a third on what the same wine would have cost you ready-bottled. Your wine merchant will arrange a preliminary tasting for you and give you the necessary advice and aid. A crew of three can cope easily. Remember that you may well find yourself 'trying' the stuff while bottling, so take care not to invite too many neighbours in to 'help', or that 300 will diminish sharply.

What to Drink with What

What	What to drink with it
Simply-flavoured dishes, hot or cold. Mild cheeses of the English variety	Inexpensive clarets like Côtes de Bourg, Côtes de Blaye, Côtes de Fronsac
Beef, lamb, pork, game, poultry, any full-blooded stuff. Stronger cheeses. Pâté. Stews	Givry, Fixin, Dôle, Monthélie, Old Algerian, Mercurey, Morgon, Moulin-à-Vent, Cornas, Lirac, Gigondas, Châteauneuf du Pape, Hermitage, Côte Rôtie, Crozes-Hermitage, St Joseph
Eggs and bacon, eggs and chips, baked beans and sausages	Any of the above, also beer, cider, Guinness, Scotch and water without ice (first-rate)
Hot and cold meats, picnic meals, or nothing at all	Any of the wines listed as going with beef, lamb, pork, etc., plus beaujolais, Beaujolais-Villages, Fleurie, Brouilly, Chiroubles

Soups	Sherry, madeira if you're feeling fancy, or the end of your apéritif provided it doesn't contain hard liquor
Oysters	Chablis, Muscadet, Guinness, Black Velvet
Fish and chips	Guinness
Curry	Beer, cider, or try a tough red chianti
Cold dishes, fish, shellfish, salads, picnics	Puligny Montrachet, Meursault, Alsace Riesling or Sylvaner, Tokay d'Alsace, Tavel Rosé (if you must), Sancerre, Pouilly Fumé, Pouilly Fuissé, a non-pricey hock or moselle
Shellfish, jellied eels, cold meats	Gewurtztraminer, Traminer
Vichyssoise, melon, before lunch	Muscat d'Alsace, Piesporter, Zeltinger
Salads, shellfish, cold buffet	Beaujolais Rosé chilled
Hot dishes not heavily spiced	Beaujolais Rosé at room temperature
Desserts, fresh fruit, especially peaches	Quarts de Chaumes, Châteaux Rieusses and Climens, Sauternes, Barsac
Fondue	Neuchâtel will help you to force it down
Anything, everything or nothing	Champagne N.V.

Abroad

I am not referring to places like Paris, where you can drink as safely as anywhere in the world, and as enjoyably too if you have £25 per day to spend on drink alone and are slow to react to insolence and cheating; nor do I mean the wine-producing areas of France or Germany, where all you need is a couple of spare livers; I mean places more apparently uncivilized, off the more remorselessly beaten-up sections of the track.

1. The presence of a labelled bottle surrounding a wine guarantees nothing. You will do as well, or as ill, and more cheaply, with the stuff out of the barrel. If you can find out what the locals go for, choose that. (A sound general rule for eats as well.)

2. Faced with a choice between bad or untrustworthy red wine on the one hand, and ditto white on the other, pick the red. In Greece, where what red there is is often sweet, pick the resinated rather than the unresinated white.

3. Smell the stuff carefully before drinking. This is not empty winemanship; the object is merely to make sure it smells of wine, and not of decaying cabbages, damp blankets, musty corks or vinegar. Not all these non-winey danger signals are unpleasant in themselves; also be on your guard against a whiff of almond or pear-drops.

4. If the red strikes you as thick, dark and heavy, feel no shame in cutting it with the local bubbly mineral water; worth trying in parts of Italy and Spain. And/or add ice. Nay, stare not so; we are not talking about vintage burgundy.

The cheaper Portuguese reds are better iced, as the locals know.

5. If you still quail, try the beer. It will arrive too cold, and will often not be very nice, but I have never heard of positive harm being done by it.

6. Those with upset guts should avoid both wine and beer. Even at their best, they irritate the large intestine. No spirit does, but stick to brands you know. Spirits made abroad are suspect, apart from brandies, fruit brandies like slivovitz and calvados, and one or two oddities like Lisbon gin. I remember, not very well, an encounter with Yugoslav Scotch ...

7. The cautious should look narrowly at all sparkling wines, except genuine French champagne, and at all sweet drinks. Still, one small glass cannot do you much harm; indeed, with some of those sparklers one sip is enough—so be even warier of ordering a whole bottle.

8. Gin men should slip a small bottle of Angostura into their luggage. You can knock together some sort of drink with it—and gin—under almost any conditions, and you can never find it abroad; well, yes, Gibraltar and Malta, perhaps.

Wine cheers the sad, revives the old, inspires the young, makes weariness forget his toil, and fear her danger, opens a new world when this, the present, palls. —LORD BYRON

The dipsomaniac and the abstainer are not only both mistaken, but they both make the same mistake. They both regard wine as a drug and not as a drink. —G. K. CHESTERTON

An aroma of damp blankets

Mean Sod's Guide

The point here is not simply to stint your guests on quality and quantity—any fool can pre-pour Moroccan red into burgundy bottles, or behave as if all knowledge of the existence of drink has been suddenly excised from his brain at 10 p.m.—but to screw them *while seeming, at any rate to their wives, to have done them rather well*. Note the limitation: your ideal objective is a quarrel on the way home between each husband and wife, he disparaging your hospitality, she saying you were very sweet and thoughtful and he is just a frustrated drunk. Points contributing to this end are marked ●.

●1. Strike at once by, on their arrival, presenting each lady with a rose and each gent with bugger-all. Rub this in by complimenting each lady on her appearance and saying in a stentorian undertone to the odd gent, 'I heard you hadn't been so well' (= pissed as a lizard every day) or 'You're looking much better than when I saw you last' (i.e. with that emperor-sized hangover).

2. Vital requirement: prepare pre- and post-dinner drinks in some undiscoverable pantry or broom-cupboard well away from the main scene. This will not only screen your niggardlinesses; it will also make the fetching of each

successive round look like a slight burden, and ●will cast an unfavourable limelight on any individual determined to wrest additional drinks out of you. Sit in a specially deep easy-chair, and practise getting out of it with a mild effort and, later in the evening, a just-audible groan, though beware of overdoing this.

3. As regards the pre-dinner period, procedures vary. The obvious one is to offer only one sort of drink, a 'cup' or 'punch' made of cheap red wine, soda water, a glass of cooking sherry if you can plunge that far, and a lot of fresh fruit to give an illusion of lavishness. Say you invented it, and add menacingly that it has more of a kick than might be expected. Serve in small glasses.

The cold-weather variant of this—same sort of wine, water, small glass of cooking brandy heated in a saucepan, pinch of nutmeg on top of each glass or mug—is more trouble, but it has two great advantages. One is that you can turn the trouble to positive account by spending nearly all your time either at the cooker, conscientiously making sure the stuff goes on being hot enough, or walking to and from the cooker—much more time than you spend actually giving people drinks. The other gain is that after a couple of doses your guests will be pouring with sweat and largely unable to take any more. (Bank up the fire or turn up the heating to aid this effect, remembering to reduce the temperature well before the kicking-out stage approaches.)

If, faced with either of these, any old-stager insists on, say, Scotch, go to your pantry and read the paper for a few minutes before filling the order. ●Hand the glass over with plenty of emphasis, perhaps bawling as you do so, 'One large Scotch whisky delivered as ordered, *sah*!'

Should you feel, as you would have reason to, that this approach is getting a little shiny with use, set your teeth and give everybody a more or less proper first drink. You can salve your pocket, however, by adding a tremendous lot of ice to fill up the glass (troublesome, but cheaper than alcohol), or, in the case of martinis, by dropping in an olive the size of a baby's fist (see *Thunderball*, by Ian Fleming, chapter 14). Cheat on later drinks as follows: in preparing a gin and tonic, for instance, put the tonic and ice and thick slice of lemon in first and pour on them a thimbleful of gin *over the back of a spoon*, so that it will linger near the surface and give a strong-tasting first sip, which is the one that counts. A friend of mine, whose mother-in-law gets a little excited after a couple of drinks, goes one better in preparing her third by pouring tonic on ice, wetting a fingertip with gin and passing it round the rim of the glass, but victims of this procedure must be selected with extreme care. Martinis should be as cold as before, but with plenty of melted ice. Whiskies are more difficult. Use the back-of-the-spoon technique with coloured glasses, or use the darkest brand you can find. Water the sherries.

4. Arrange dinner early, and see that the food is plentiful, however cheap it is. You can get away with not serving wine with the first course, no matter what it may be. When the main course is on the table, 'suddenly realize' you have not opened the wine, and proceed to do so now with a lot of cork-popping. The wine itself will not, of course, be French or German; let us call it Ruritanian Gold Label. Pour it with ceremony, explaining that you and your wife (●especially she) 'fell in love with it' on holiday there and will be 'interested' in people's reactions. When these turn out to consist of polite, or barely polite, silence, *either* say nostalgically that to appreciate it perhaps you have to have drunk a lot of it with that marvellous local food under that sun, etc., *or* announce bluffly, 'Doesn't travel, does it? Doesn't travel.' Judge your audience.

5. Sit over the remains of dinner as long as you dare or

can bear to, then take the company off to the drawing-room and make great play with doling out coffee. By this stage (a vague, prolonged one anyhow), a good half-hour of abrupt and total forgetfulness about the very idea of drink can profitably be risked. At its end, 'suddenly realize' you have imposed a drought and offer brandy, explaining a good deal less than half apologetically that you have no cognac, only a 'rather exceptional' armagnac. This, of course, produced with due slowness from your pantry, is a watered-down cooking brandy from remote parts of France or from South Africa—a just-potable that will already, did they but know it, be familiar to those of your guests who have drunk 'armagnac' at the average London restaurant.* ●Ask the ladies if they would care to try a glass of Strelsauvada, a 'rather obscure' Ruritanian liqueur made from rotten figs with almond-skin flavouring which admittedly can 'play you up' if you are not used to it. They will all say no and think highly of you for the offer.

6. Play out time with groan-preceded, tardily produced, ice-crammed Scotches, remembering the recourse of saying loudly, ●'I find *myself* that a glass of cold *beer* [out of the cheapest quart bottles from the pub] is the best thing *at this time of night*.'

7. Along the lines of sticking more fruit than any sane person could want in the pre-dinner 'punch' or 'cup', put out a lot of pseudo-luxuries like flood-damaged truncheon-sized cigars, bulk-bought ●after-dinner mints, bankrupt-stock ●vari-coloured cigarettes, etc.

8. Your own drinks. These must obviously not be allowed to fall below any kind of accustomed level, how-

* The more sophisticated, and troublesome, method, much used in restaurants, is to take a couple of handfuls of raisins, split them open, put them in a basin, pour some lousy brandy over them and leave for twenty-four hours. Strain and serve as, probably, a little-known cognac rather than armagnac.

ever cruel the deprivations you force on your guests. You will naturally refresh yourself with periodic nips in your pantry, but going thither at all often may make undesirable shags think, even say, that you ought to be bringing thence a drink for them. So *either* choose between a darkly tinted glass ('an old friend of mine in Venice gave it me— apparently it's rather valuable, ha ha ha') and a silver cup of some sort ('actually it's my christening-mug from T. S. Eliot—believe it or not, ha ha ha)', which you stick inseparably to and can undetectably fill with neat whisky, *or* boldly use a plain glass containing one of those light-coloured blends known, at any rate in the U.S.A., as a 'husband's Scotch'—'Why, hell, Mamie, just take a look; you can see it's near as a damn pure water,' and hell, Jim, Jack, Joe and the rest of the crowd.

9. If you think that all or most of the above is mere satirical fantasy, you cannot have been around much yet.

Mean Slag's Guide

The following menu is intended only as an example. Remember that there must be plenty of everything, and that the hot dishes must be hot, so as to forestall a couple of obvious complaints. ● The mean sod can help by making faces and vague noises at a couple of wives to suggest that the mean slag is at a difficult time of the month.

> *Petits pains et beurre*
> *Pouding de Yorkshire*
> *Spaghetti poco bolognese*
> *Boeuf à bon marché*
> *Pommes bouillies*
> *Navets vieux*
> *Salade de fruits sans sucre*
> *Café*

Notes. (i) A good ten minutes with no food in sight but rolls and butter will, as restaurants know, take the edge off most appetites.

(ii) Explain that in your native Wales they often start a meal with plain Yorkshire pudding, and hint that it is a particularly working-class dish in order to appease, or at least silence, any lefties in the company.

(iii) This is just spaghetti with not nearly enough sauce.

(iv) If, after this broadside of almost unrelieved starch, any of your guests are still afloat, roast stewing beef with boiled potatoes and old turnips (new ones are very nice if properly done) should finish them off. The no doubt considerable unconsumed portion of the beef can be curried next day.

(v) Leaving all sugar out of a fruit salad built mainly on fresh pineapple and oranges will make it virtually un-eatable. You cannot actually refuse to provide sugar if asked, but there is a good chance that, in their beaten state, your guests will not raise the matter. As before, the left-overs can be rescued next day.

(vi) Must be fresh, and the process of making should be the most elaborate and lengthy and hitch-prone that can be found, with as much of it as possible taking place in front of the guests. It is a job for sod rather than slag, for while he is fiddling with the coffee he obviously cannot be pour-ing drinks, and there is ● value there too.

A little-known Central American liquor: 'Cassiri ... the local drink made of fermented cassava [a root vegetable].' He drank some and handed the bowl to Tony. It con-tained a thick, purplish fluid. When Tony had drunk a little, Dr Messinger explained, 'It is made in an interesting way. The women chew the root up and spit it into a hollow tree-trunk'. —EVELYN WAUGH

87

The Hangover

What a subject! And, in very truth, for once, a 'strangely neglected' one. Oh, I know you can hardly open a newspaper or magazine without coming across a set of instructions—most of them unoriginal, some of them quite unhelpful and one or two of them actually harmful—on how to cure this virtually pandemic ailment. But such discussions concentrate exclusively on physical manifestations, as if one were treating a mere illness. They omit altogether the psychological, moral, emotional, spiritual aspects: all that vast, vague, awful, shimmering metaphysical superstructure that makes the hangover a (fortunately) unique route to self-knowledge and self-realization.

Imaginative literature is not much better. There are poems and songs about drinking, of course, but none to speak of about getting drunk, let alone having been drunk. Novelists go into the subject more deeply and extensively, but tend to straddle the target, either polishing off the hero's hangover in a few sentences or, so to speak, making it the whole of the novel. In the latter case, the hero will almost certainly be a dipsomaniac, who is not as most men are and never less so than on the morning after. This vital difference, together with much else, is firmly brought out in Charles Jackson's marvellous and horrifying *The Lost Weekend*, still the best fictional account of alcoholism I have read.

The morning after the night before ...

A few writers can be taken as metaphorically illuminating the world of the hangover while ostensibly dealing with something else. Parts of Dostoevsky can be read in this way. Some of Poe's Tales convey perfectly the prevailing gloomy uneasiness and sudden fits of outlandish dread so many of us could recognize, and Poe himself had a drink problem; contrary to popular belief, he was not a dipsomaniac, but his system was abnormally intolerant of alcohol, so that just a couple of slugs would lay him on his back, no doubt with a real premature-burial of a hangover to follow. Perhaps Kafka's story *The Metamorphosis*, which starts with the hero waking up one morning and finding he has turned into a man-sized cockroach, is the best literary treatment of all. The central image could hardly be better chosen, and there is a telling touch in the nasty way everybody goes on at the chap. (I can find no information about Kafka's drinking history.)

It is not my job, or anyway I absolutely decline, to attempt a full, direct description of the metaphysical hangover: no fun to write or read. But I hope something of this will emerge by implication from my list of counter-measures. Before I get on to that, however, I must deal with the physical hangover, which is in any case the logical one to tackle first, and the dispersal of which will notably alleviate the other—mind and body, as we have already seen, being nowhere more intimately connected than in the sphere of drink. Here, then, is how to cope with

THE PHYSICAL HANGOVER

1. Immediately on waking, start telling yourself how lucky you are to be feeling so bloody awful. This, known as George Gale's Paradox, recognizes the truth that if you do *not* feel bloody awful after a hefty night then you are still

drunk, and must sober up in a waking state before hangover dawns.

2. If your wife or other partner is beside you, and (of course) is willing, perform the sexual act as vigorously as you can. The exercise will do you good, and—on the assumption that you enjoy sex—you will feel toned up emotionally, thus delivering a hit-and-run raid on your metaphysical hangover (M.H.) before you formally declare war on it.

Warnings. (i) If you are in bed with somebody you should not be in bed with, and have *in the least degree* a bad conscience about this, abstain. Guilt and shame are prominent constituents of the M.H., and will certainly be sharpened by indulgence on such an occasion.

(ii) For the same generic reason, do not take the matter into your own hands if you awake by yourself.

3. Having of course omitted to drink all that water before retiring, drink a lot of it now, more than you need to satisfy your immediate thirst. Alcohol is a notorious dehydrant, and a considerable part of your physical hangover (P.H.) comes from the lack of water in your cells.

At this point I must assume that you can devote at least a good part of the day to yourself and your condition. Those who inescapably have to get up and do something can only stay in bed as long as they dare, get up, shave, take a hot bath or shower (more of this later), breakfast off an unsweetened grapefruit (m.o.t.l.) and coffee, and clear off, with the intention of getting as drunk at lunchtime as they dare. Others can read on—but let me just observe in passing that the reason why so many professional artists drink a lot is not necessarily very much to do with the artistic temperament, etc. It is simply that they can afford to, because they can normally take a large part of a day off to deal with the ravages. So, then,

4. Stay in bed until you can stand it no longer. Simple fatigue is another great constituent of the P.H.

5. Refrain at all costs from taking a cold shower. It may bring temporary relief, but in my own and others' experience it will give your M.H. a tremendous boost after about half an hour, in extreme cases making you feel like a creature from another planet. Perhaps this is the result of having dealt another shock to your already shocked system. The ideal arrangement, very much worth the trouble and expense if you are anything of a serious drinker, is a shower fixed over the bath. Run a bath as hot as you can bear and lie in it as long as you can bear. When it becomes too much, stand up and have a hot shower, then lie down again and repeat the sequence. This is time well spent.

Warning. Do not do this unless you are quite sure your heart and the rest of you will stand it. I would find it most disagreeable to be accused of precipitating your death, especially in court.

6. Shave. A drag, true, and you may well cut yourself, but it is a calming exercise and will lift your morale (another sideswipe at your M.H.).

7. Whatever the state of your stomach, do not take an alkalizing agent such as bicarbonate of soda. There is some of this in most hangover remedies but not enough to do you any harm, and the bubbling is cheerful. Better to take unsweetened fruit juice or a grapefruit without sugar. The reasoning behind this, known as Philip Hope-Wallace's Syndrome, is that your stomach, on receiving a further dose of acid, will say to itself, 'Oh, I see: we need more alkaline,' and proceed to neutralize itself. Bicarbonate will make it say, 'Oh, I see: we need more acid,' and do you further damage.

If you find this unconvincing, take heed of what happened one morning when, with a kingly hangover, I took bicarbonate with a vodka chaser. My companion said 'Let's see what's happening in your stomach,' and poured the remnant of the vodka into the remnant of the bicarbonate solution. The mixture turned black and gave off smoke.

8. Eat nothing, or nothing else. Give your digestion the morning off. You may drink coffee, though do not expect this to do anything for you beyond making you feel more wide-awake.

9. Try not to smoke. That nicotine has contributed to your P.H. is a view held by many people, including myself.

10. By now you will have shot a good deal of the morning. Get through the rest of it somehow, avoiding the society of your fellows. Talk is tiring. Go for a walk, or sit or lie about in the fresh air. At eleven or so, see if you fancy the idea of a Polish Bison (hot Bovril and vodka). It is still worth while without the vodka. You can start working on your M.H. any time you like.

11. About 12.30, firmly take a hair (or better, in Cyril Connolly's phrase, a tuft) of the dog that bit you. The dog, by the way, is of no particular breed: there is no obligation to go for the same drink as the one you were mainly punishing the night before. Many will favour the Bloody Mary, though see my remarks on this in the Drinks section. Others swear by the Underburg. For the ignorant, this is a highly alcoholic bitters rather resembling Fernet Branca, but in my experience more usually effective. It comes in miniature bottles holding about a pub double, and should be put down in one. The effect on one's insides, after a few seconds, is rather like that of throwing a cricket-ball into an empty bath, and the resulting mild convulsions and cries of shock are well worth witnessing. But thereafter a comforting glow supervenes, and very often a marked turn for the better. By now, one way or another, you will be

readier to face the rest of mankind and a convivial lunch-time can well result. Eat what you like within reason, avoiding anything greasy or rich. If your P.H. is still with you afterwards, go to bed.

Before going on to the M.H., I will, for completeness' sake, mention three supposed hangover cures, all described as infallible by those who told me about them, though I have not tried any of the three. The first two are hard to come by.

12. Go down the mine on the early-morning shift at the coal-face.

13. Go up for half an hour in an open aeroplane, needless to say with a non-hungover person at the controls.

14. Known as Donald Watt's Jolt, this consists of a tumbler of some sweet liqueur, Bénédictine or Grand Marnier, taken in lieu of breakfast. Its inventor told me that with one of them inside him he once spent three-quarters of an hour at a freezing bus-stop 'without turning a hair'. It is true that the sugar in the drink will give you energy and the alcohol alcohol.

At this point, younger readers may relax the unremitting attention with which they have followed the above. They are mostly strangers to the M.H. But they will grin or jeer at their peril. Let them rest assured that, as they grow older, the M.H. will more and more come to fill the gap left by their progressively less severe P.H. And, of the two, incomparably the more dreadful is

THE METAPHYSICAL HANGOVER

1. Deal thoroughly with your P.H.
2. When that ineffable compound of depression, sadness

(these tow are not the same), anxiety, self-hatred, sense of failure and fear for the future begins to steal over you, start telling yourself that what you have is a hangover. You are not sickening for anything, you have not suffered a minor brain lesion, you are not all that bad at your job, your family and friends are not leagued in a conspiracy of barely maintained silence about what a shit you are, you have not come at last to see life as it really is, and there is no use crying over spilt milk. If this works, if you can convince yourself, you need do no more, as provided in the markedly philosophical

 G.P. 9: *He who truly believes he has a hangover has no hangover.*

3. If necessary, then, embark on *either* the M.H. Literature Course *or* the M.H. Music Course *or* both in succession (not simultaneously). Going off and gazing at some painting, building or bit of statuary might do you good too, but most people, I think, will find such things unimmediate for this—perhaps any—purpose. The structure of both Courses, HANGOVER READING and HANGOVER LISTENING, rests on the principle that you must feel worse emotionally before you start to feel better. A good cry is the initial aim.

HANGOVER READING

Begin with verse, if you have any taste for it. Any really gloomy stuff that you admire will do. My own choice would tend to include the final scene of *Paradise Lost*, Book XII, lines 606 to the end, with what is probably the most poignant moment in all our literature coming at lines 624-6. The trouble here, though, is that today of all days you do not want to be reminded of how inferior you are to the man next door, let alone to a chap like Milton. Safer to pick somebody less horribly great. I would plump for the poems of A. E. Housman and/or R. S. Thomas, not that they are in the least interchangeable. Matthew Arnold's *Sohrab and Rustum* is good, too, if a little long for the purpose.

Switch to prose with the same principles of selection. I suggest Alexander Solzhenitsyn's *One Day in the Life of Ivan Denisovich*. It is not gloomy exactly, but its picture of life in a Russian labour camp will do you the important service of suggesting that there are plenty of people about who have a bloody sight more to put up with than you (or I) have or ever will have, and who put up with it, if not cheerfully, at any rate in no mood of self-pity.

Turn now to stuff that suggests there may be some point to living after all. Battle poems come in rather well here: Macaulay's *Horatius*, for instance. Or, should you feel that this selection is getting a bit British (for the Roman virtues Macaulay celebrates have very much that sort of flavour), try Chesterton's *Lepanto*. The naval victory in 1571 of the forces of the Papal League over the Turks and their allies was accomplished without the assistance of a single Anglo-Saxon (or Protestant). Try not to mind the way Chesterton makes some play with the fact that this was a victory of Christians over Moslems.

By this time you could well be finding it conceivable that you might smile again some day. However, defer funny stuff for the moment. Try a good thriller or action story, which will start to wean you from self-observation and the darker emotions: Ian Fleming, Eric Ambler, Gavin Lyall, Dick Francis, Geoffrey Household, C. S. Forester (perhaps the most useful of the lot). Turn to comedy only after that; but it must be white—i.e. not black—comedy: P. G. Wodehouse, Stephen Leacock,

Captain Marryat, Anthony Powell (not Evelyn Waugh), Peter De Vries (not *The Blood of the Lamb*, which, though very funny, has its real place in the tearful category, and a distinguished one). I am not suggesting that these writers are comparable in other ways than that they make unwillingness to laugh seem a little pompous and absurd.

HANGOVER LISTENING

Here, the trap is to set your sights too high. On the argument tentatively advanced against unduly great literature, give a wide berth to anyone like Mozart. Go for someone who is merely a towering genius. Tchaikovsky would be my best buy in this department, and his Sixth Symphony (the *Pathétique*) my individual selection. After various false consolations have been set aside, its last movement really does what the composer intended and, in an amazingly non-dreary way, evokes total despair: sonic M.H. if ever I heard it.

Alternatively, or next, try Tchaikovsky's successor, Sibelius. *The Swan of Tuonela* comes to mind, often recommended though it curiously is (or was in my youth) as a seduction background-piece. (Scope for a little article there.) Better still for our purpose, I think, is the same composer's incidental music to Maeterlinck's play, *Pelléas and Mélisande*: not to be confused with Debussy's opera of that name. The last section of the Sibelius, in particular, carries the ever-so-slightly phoney and overdone pathos that is exactly what you want in your present state.

If you can stand vocal music, I strongly recommend Brahms's *Alto Rhapsody*—not an alto sax, you peasant, but a contralto voice, with men's choir and full orchestra. By what must be pure chance, the words sung, from a— between you and me, rather crappy—poem of Goethe's,

Harzreise im Winter, sound like an only slightly metaphorical account of a hangover. They begin, '*Aber abseits wer ist's?*'—all right, I am only copying it off the record-sleeve; they begin, 'But who is that (standing) apart? His path is lost in the undergrowth,' and end with an appeal to God to 'open the clouded vista over the thousand springs beside the thirsty one in the desert.' That last phrase gets a lot in. You can restore some of your fallen dignity by telling yourself that you too are a *Duerstender in der Wueste*. This is a piece that would fetch tears from a stone, especially a half-stoned stone, and nobody without a record of it in his possession should dare to say that he likes music. The Kathleen Ferrier version is still unequalled after twenty years.

Turn now to something lively and extrovert, but be careful. Quite a lot of stuff that appears to be so at first inspection has a nasty habit of sneaking in odd blows to the emotional solar plexus; ballet music (except Tchaikovsky) and overtures to light operas and such are safer—Suppé, if you have no objection to being reminded of school sports days here and there, is fine. Or better, Haydn's Trumpet Concerto, which would make a zombie dance.

Jazz is not much good for your M.H., and pop will probably worsen your P.H. But if you really feel that life could not possibly be gloomier, try any slow Miles Davis track. It will suggest to you that, however gloomy life may be, it cannot possibly be as gloomy as Davis makes it out to be. There is also the likely bonus to be gained from hearing some bystander refer to Davis as Miles instead of Davis. The surge of adrenalin at this piece of trendy pseudo-familiarity will buck up your system, and striking the offender to the ground will restore your belief in your own masculinity, rugged force, etc.
Warning: Make quiet sure that Davis's sometime partner,

John Coltrane, is not 'playing' his saxophone on any track you choose. *He* will suggest to you, in the strongest terms, that life is exactly what you are at present taking it to be: cheap, futile and meaningless.

Wine maketh merry: but money answereth all things. — ECCLESIASTES

THREE NOTABLE BREAKFASTS

Sir Winston Churchill's
1 brace cold snipe
1 pint port

Horatio Bottomley's
1 pair kippers
1 tumbler brandy and water

Samuel Taylor Coleridge's (Sundays only)
6 fried eggs
1 glass laudanum* and seltzer†

   * Alcoholic tincture of opium.
   † An effervescent mineral water.

I never tasted [whisky], except once for experiment at the inn at Inverary ... It was strong but not pungent ... What was the process I had no opportunity of inquiring, nor do I wish to improve the art of making poison pleasant.

SAMUEL JOHNSON

The Boozing Man's Diet

The first, indeed the only, requirement of a diet is that if should lose you weight *without reducing your alcoholic intake by the smallest degree*. Well, and it should be simple: no charts, tables, menus, recipes. None of those pages of fusspottery which normally end—*end*, after you have wasted minutes ploughing your way through—'and, of course, no alcohol' in tones of fatuous apology for laying tongue to something so pikestaff-plain. Of *course*? No *alcohol*? What kind of people do they think we are?

This diet took over a stone off me in three months, or what would have been three months if I had not often backslid with a curry or a fruit pie. That is about as fast a rate of loss as is medically desirable, which reminds me to say that you will consult your physician before embarking on the regime. No one, including no one's widow, is going to be able to sue me for having brought about a case of scurvy, osteitis deformans, alcoholic poisoning, diabetes, beri-beri or any other illness, disease or malady of any kind or sort whatsoever.

The scheme rests on

🙟G.P. 10: *Eating fattens you.*

'What, no drink?'

Nearly all diets start with the exclusion of bread, potatoes and sugar. This one goes on to exclude vegetables and fruit as well, or nearly. But remember, remember that drink is in. Here is

YOUR DAY'S FOOD

Breakfast is a whole grapefruit eaten without sugar, or, if you must, with artificial sweetener. Tea or coffee with the same sweetener if required. One boiled egg if you honestly have a long morning to get through. No bread or toast—and that goes for that bit of crust off your wife's toast. Drop it this minute, I say!

Lunch and dinner consist of a selection of thin soup, eggs, fish of all kinds, meat, poultry, game, etc., and cheese, laced with mustard and Worcester sauce. No thick sauces or pickles. Tea or coffee as required. Eat as much salt as you like. Some diets disrecommend this, on the grounds that salt causes the body to retain fluids and so in effect makes you heavier. This is true but ludicrous, unless you are so titanic that an extra few ounces will kill you as you rise from your chair. As well lose weight by donating blood or having your hair cut.

Notes. (i) Pick a sweetener combining saccharine with a little sugar for palatability's sake. Consult your chemist.

(ii) The point of the mustard and Worcester sauce is partly that you must have something to eke out the bareness of what you are allowed, and partly that both of them irritate the large intestine, giving the laxative effect you will need with a reduced food intake. Onions (avoid fried ones) will assist here.

(iii) Another substantial advantage of the diet is that you can stick pretty closely to it even when eating out, a testing time for diets. But, unless you fancy spending most of the meal discussing your weight problem with the company, say that your new-found aversion to vegetables, fruit, thick sauces and the rest springs from psychiatric advice or a religious conversion, either of which you prefer not to go into now.

(iv) Another eating-out tip, applying to restaurants: order a dish you hate or one you know they do badly. After a few mouthfuls of the average chicken à la Kiev or boeuf Stroganoff—two of my own unfavourites—your appetite will be fully satisfied. Make the waiter leave your plate in front of you while your companions' gâteaux, crêpes suzette and so on are being ordered and consumed.

YOUR DAY'S DRINK

is a much more cheerful topic. Although your intake of alcohol will, as promised, remain undiminished, there are kinds of drink you should do your best to cultivate and give the go-by to respectively, as follows:

1. Keep your wines and fortified wines as dry as you can. However much nicer it may be, a Sauternes is more fattening than a white burgundy. Similarly, stay off sweet liqueurs, a policy which will, as noted, also help your hangover problem.

2. Avoid non-alcoholic additives, apart from water and soda. Slimmers' tonic water may well be less damaging to your figure than the ordinary kind, but I have conducted no controlled experiments in this field. Juices, especially tomato juice, are great fatteners.

3. Drink diabetic or low-calorie beer; so much the better if you can substitute some for your apéritif or after-dinner drink. There is an excellent one called Diat Pils

(short for Pilsner, not pills) obtainable through some off-licences and groceries or direct from Holsten Distributors Ltd, 63 Southwark Park Road, London SE16. There are shags who would attack this brew as artificial, non-authentic, etc., on which point consult G.P. 7 and ignore them. Diat Pils is very adequately alcoholic, pleasant to the eye, at least as tasty as most ordinary beers, and totally wholesome: approved, indeed, by the British Diabetic Association. It is admittedly a bit pricey, but, to my mind, worth every penny.

4. Alcohol science is full of crap. It will tell you, for instance, that drink does not really warm you up, it only makes you feel warm—oh, I see; and it will go on about alcohol being not a stimulant but a depressant, which turns out to mean that it depresses qualities like shyness and self-criticism, and so makes you behave as if you had been stimulated—thanks. In the same style, the said science will maintain that alcohol does not really fatten you, it only sets in train a process at the end of which you weigh more. Nevertheless, strong drink does, more than anything else taken by mouth, apart from stuff like cement, cram on the poundage. If you can face it, if you really want to be shapelier faster, if you are dissatisfied with zipping up your trousers at 45 degrees instead of vertically, cut down on hard liquor. Doing so will carry the bonus of—dare I say it?—conducing to your general health.

Such power hath Beer. The heart which grief hath canker'd
Hath one unfailing remedy —the Tankard.
CHARLES STUART CALVERLEY

How Not to Get Drunk

This is strictly two topics—how to keep sober (or at least relatively in control) at a drinking party, and what to avoid with the morning after in mind—but they overlap so much in practice that I will treat them under the same heading.

Staying away altogether is a stratagem sometimes facetiously put forward at the outset of such discussions as these. To move at once to the realm of the practical, *eating* has much to be said for it. As well as retarding (though not preventing) the absorption of alcohol, food will slow up your drinking rate, not just because most people put their glasses down while actually chewing, but because you are now satisfying your appetite by eating rather than drinking: hunger makes you drink more than you otherwise would. According to some, oily foods are the most effective soakers-up of the drink already in your stomach, but others point to the risk of upsetting a digestion already under alcoholic attack.

There is a great deal of folklore about *taking some olive oil or milk* before joining the party. This will indeed retard absorption of alcohol, but, as before, it will all get to you in the end. Do not, in any case, overdo the fatty prelude. An acquaintance of mine, led astray by quantitative thinking, once started the evening with a tumbler of olive oil, following this up with a dozen or so whiskies. These, after a couple of hours of nibbling at the film of mucilage supposedly lining his stomach, finally broke through in a body and laid him on the floor of the saloon bar of the Metropole Hotel, Swansea, fortunately after I had left. I would be chary of this tactic. The principle does, however, work well the other way round. In the middle of a greasy meal, a quick neat double brandy certainly seems to hose down your stomach wall and give you heart and strength to continue eating.

Diluting your drinks sounds a good idea to many, and will help to reverse the dehydration that all alcohol brings, so that you will be better off next day. But, again, the alcohol itself will get to you in full. Nor is it true (in my experience, at least) that a double Scotch, say, diluted with a lot of soda takes longer to put down than the same with a little, so reducing your effective intake. The opposite of all this is truer. Spirits distilled out at 70° British proof, which are what you will usually meet, are too strong in the neat state to be wholly absorbed by the system; a proportion is eventually passed without ever having reached you. Dilution with just less than an equal amount of water is the point at which all the alcohol will enter your bloodstream—a fact known, without benefit of science, to Scotch and Irish drinkers for two centuries. So, in fact, spirit-bibbers should try *drinking neat un-iced spirits*, a practice so gruelling that their actual intake is almost bound to drop too.

I pass over such unhelpful prescriptions as *being tall and fat*; it is nevertheless true that your degree of drunkenness depends on a proportion between how much you drink and how large a frame you have to spread it over, with the result that big men, other things being equal, can take more than small men. Other things, of course, never are equal, though there is not much that can be done about them either. *Not being tired, not being depressed, not being specially elated* — these and other negative states will also stiffen your resistance to alcohol, but I know they do not descend at will. It can be said, however, not very cheeringly, that you should watch your drinking rate when you are tired, depressed, etc., (in fact always, because x drinks drunk in y minutes are more potent than x drinks drunk in $2y$ minutes).

Fatigue is an important element in the hangover, too. Alcohol gives you energy, or, what is hard to distinguish from it, the illusion of energy, and under its influence you will stand for hours at a stretch, throw yourself about, do exhausting imitations, perhaps fight a bit, even, God help you, dance. This will burn up a little alcohol, true, but you will pay for it next morning. A researcher is supposed once to have measured out two identical doses of drink, put the first lot down at a full-scale party and the second, some evenings later, at home with a book, smoking the same number of cigarettes on each occasion and going to bed at the same time. Result, big hangover and no hangover respectively. *Sitting down whenever possible*, then, will help you, and so, *a fortiori*, will *resisting the temptation to dance*, should you be subject to such impulses.

An equally unsurprising way of avoiding fatigue is *going to bed in reasonable time*, easily said, I know, but more easily done, too, if you allow the soporific effects of drink to run their natural course. This means staying away from stimulants, and that means *avoiding coffee*, both on its own and with liquor poured into it: the latter, by holding you up with one hand while it pastes you at leisure with the other, is the most solidly dependable way I know of ensuring a fearful tomorrow. Hostesses, especially, should take note of this principle, and cut out those steaming midnight mugs which, intended to send the company cheerfully on its way, so often set the tongues wagging and the Scotch circulating again.

Avoiding things can hardly help coming up more than once in the present connection. To proceed, then: *avoiding very strong drinks* is more than the piece of padding it may seem. The alcoholic strength or proof of a wine, spirit, etc., is not a straightforward index of its power to intoxicate. The relationship is non-linear, or, if you must have everything spelt out, the graph plotting proof against kick is not straight. Above the standard strength of spirits it bends sharply upward, so that for instance green Chartreuse, which is distilled out at 96° proof, is not just a bit over a third as strong again as, say, a gin at 70°, but several times stronger in its effect.

I once shared a half-litre bottle of Polish Plain Spirit (140° proof) with two chums. I only spoke twice, first to say, 'Cut out that laughing—it can't have got to you yet,' and not all that much later to say, 'I think I'll go to bed now.'

Hand in hand with this warning comes one about *avoiding sweet drinks*. These play hell with you next day; I forget why, but I remember how. So go carefully, at least, with Southern Comfort, a delicious compound of old bourbon whiskey, oranges and peaches that tips the scales at 87·7° proof.

Avoiding unfamiliar drinks is my final interdiction. Here, again, I mean more than just steering clear of Malagasy malaga, St Peter Port port-type and such, at any rate when you are not in a mood of pure curiosity and cold sober. A friend reports seeing a Highland sergeant, weaned on a bottle of Scotch a day, pass out in his chair after his first-ever half-dozen glasses of table wine. I asked if he was shamming, and was told that his mates were kissing his girl over his recumbent form, which was felt to clinch matters. It is as if—and in the always subjective, idiosyncratic context of drink it need only be as if—body and mind together develop a tolerance to your usual potation, a kind of self-conferred immunity. Do not test this hypothesis too rigorously.

I suppose I cannot leave this topic without reciting the old one about *drinking a lot of water and taking aspirin and/or stomach powders before you finally retire*. It is a pretty useless one as well as an old one because, although the advice is perfectly sound, you will find next morning that you have not followed it. Alternatively, anyone who can summon the will and the energy and the powers of reflection called for has not reached the state in which he really needs the treatment.

After all these bans and discouragements I will throw in one crumb, or tot, of comfort. I am nearly (yes, nearly) sure that mixing your drinks neither makes you drunker nor gives you a worse time the following day than if you had taken the equivalent dosage in some single form of alcohol. After three dry martinis and two sherries and two glasses of hock and four of burgundy and one of Sauternes and two of claret and three of port and two brandies and three whiskies-and-soda and a beer, most men will be very drunk and will have a very bad hangover. But might not the quantity be at work here? An evening when you drink a great deal will also be one when you mix them.

Well—if you want to behave better and feel better, the only absolutely certain method is *drinking less*. But to find out how to do *that*, you will have to find a more expert expert than I shall ever be.

When a man commits a crime under what is miscalled the 'influence' of drink, he should, where possible, be punished double—once for the bad act, and once for the misuse of the good thing, by forcing it to reveal his true nature. —GEORGE SAINTSBURY

Other Panthers For Your Enjoyment

Fictional Diversions

☐ **Violette Leduc**   **LA BATARDE**   **60p**
In this famous autobiographical novel a great writer lays bare the
secrets of her checkered life and her loves – largely for other
women.

☐ **Violette Leduc**   **RAVAGES**   **50p**
'Violette Leduc has a wonderful feeling for all kinds of sensual
happiness' – *Daily Mail*. A novel with all the candour and
poignancy of LA BATARDE.

☐ **Angus Stewart**   **SANDEL**   **30p**
The well-reviewed novel of a young man's relationship with a boy.
'A controlled and beautifully written love story, at once
passionate and pure' – *New Statesman*

☐ **Henri Barbusse**   **HELL**   **30p**
Life in a Parisian girl's bedsitter viewed through a hole in the wall by
her next door neighbour, an impoverished and struggling young
student. Cold, French realism working at its coldest. By the famous
author of *Under Fire*.

☐ **Maureen Duffy**   **WOUNDS**   **30p**
A man and a woman making love: tenderly they explore each
other's body and mind. No taboos, no shame. Flesh is there to be
caressed, thoughts to be exchanged. But – outside this sensual, very
private world the world is harsh. This story of pain and pleasure
has an honesty rare in contemporary fiction. *Here*, says the author,
is where life inflicts its wounds.

☐ **Kingsley Amis**   **I WANT IT NOW**   **35p**
A poor little rich girl, Simona, and a TV interviewer, Ronnie,
meet, merge, and strive for the things that *they* want tout de
suite. In a word, that knowing, sardonic Amis is at it again in
another bestselling high comedy. 'Wickedly entertaining' –
Sunday Times

Highly-Praised Modern Novels

☐ **John Fowles**   **THE FRENCH LIEUTENANT'S WOMAN**   **50p**

Although Fowles is an English – and *how* – writer his novel has been on the American bestseller lists for months. To read it is an experience. 'When the book's one sexual encounter takes place it's so explosive it nearly blows the top of your head off' – *New York Saturday Review*

☐ **David Caute**   **THE DECLINE OF THE WEST**   **60p**

A newly independent African state in bloody turmoil, and the world's adventurers – male and female – home in like vultures. Strong reading.

☐ **John Barth**   **THE SOT-WEED FACTOR**   **75p**

The story of a mid-eighteenth century man of fortune, told in a modern spirit by one of America's great writers. 'Most magnificent, totally scandalous' – Patrick Campbell, *The Sunday Times*

☐ **Elizabeth Bowen**   **EVA TROUT**   **35p**

'Elizabeth Bowen is a splendid artist, intelligent, generous and acutely aware, who has been telling her readers for years that love is a necessity, and that its loss or absence is the greatest tragedy man knows' – *Financial Times*

☐ **Norman Mailer**   **THE NAKED AND THE DEAD**   **60p**

The greatest novel from world war two.

☐ **Mordecai Richler**   **COCKSURE**   **40p**

Constantly reprinted by public demand. The brilliant satiric picture of a tycoon whose business and sexual appetites know no limits.

Obtainable from all booksellers and newsagents. If you have any difficulty please send purchase price plus 7p postage per book to Panther Cash Sales, P.O. Box 11, Falmouth, Cornwall.

I enclose a cheque/postal order for titles ticked above plus 7p. a book to cover postage and packing.

Name _____

Address _____

_____